ORCHID GROWING
— *In The Tropics* —

ORCHID GROWING
— *In The Tropics* —

Orchid Society of South East Asia

(Singapore)

TIMES EDITIONS

Orchid Growing in the Tropics

Times Editions Pte Ltd
1 New Industrial Road
Singapore 1953

Times Subang
Lot 46, Subang Hi-Tech Industrial Park
40000 Shah Alam
Selangor Darul Ehsan
Malaysia

Colour separation by Magenta Lithographic Consultants
Printed by Kim Hup Lee Printing Co Pte Ltd

ISBN 981 204 108 7

Contents

Acknowledgements

An edited book of this nature inevitably benefits from the efforts of many, and the editor's list of acknowledgements has to be a long one.

Part of the chapter texts were contributed by Koay Sim Huat (viruses); A. C. Leong (pests and diseases, seedlings); Ng Huang Gieh (pests and diseases); Phoon Yoon Seng (choosing and buying, showing); and Whang Lay Keng (seedlings). Jassy Quek-Phua Lek Kheng, Koh-Low Neok Chein and Woon Mui Hwang, all of the Singapore Botanic Gardens, supplied all the text for sterile culture techniques. George Alphonso, former Director, Singapore Botanic Gardens, kindly made published material available for reference.

I am grateful for comments on chapter texts by George Alphonso, Yusof Alsagoff, David Lim, James Mok, Phoon Yoon Seng, Richard Sng, Kiat Tan, Peggy Tan and Yoke-Lan Wicks. Especially detailed and therefore useful comments came from Harold Johnson and A. C. Leong. Tim Yam gave invaluable help with checking hybrid names and parentages. Many other useful suggestions were made by more members of OSSEA than can be mentioned here, and all these are gratefully acknowledged. The actual business of writing the bulk of the book and translating comments, material and ideas into a complete text fell to myself; I therefore bear the responsibility for any errors or omissions that have been perpetrated, despite the efforts of everyone else to get things right.

The structure and conception of the book owes much to Dr Kiat Tan, Executive Director, Singapore Botanic Gardens, who originally thought up the idea of approaching growing through descriptions of cultivation regimes. His support, and that of his staff at the Gardens, was essential and is gratefully acknowledged here. I must also thank here Syed Yusof Alsagoff, OSSEA President over the whole period of the preparation of this book, for his unflagging support of the whole enterprise, and for his faith in my ability to get it done. Particular thanks are due to Peggy Tan for many hours of effort put in considering what kind of book it was to be, and, by drafting layouts, showing me what was possible.

I must express also gratitude mingled with some apology to Barbara Fuller, who edited the book for Times Editions, and who had to cope with my reluctance to commit myself to firm deadlines. I should also like to add a word of thanks to my long-suffering family, for tolerating this project hanging over their heads, as well as mine, for so long.

John Elliott
Editor

Preface

This book is written for the novice orchid grower. It deals specifically with orchid growing in tropical conditions, especially tropical lowlands. It does not assume prior experience, nor does it assume the reader has a large garden. On the contrary, it specifically includes suggestions on how orchids may be grown on balconies.

The book is based on the experience of members of the Orchid Society of South East Asia. OSSEA members have been growing orchids since the Society was founded as the Malayan Orchid Society in 1928, and have bred and registered many new hybrids. However, the Society has never previously published a comprehensive guide to growing, despite the need for such a book. In doing so now, it is proper to remember the contribution of the founders of orchid growing to both private and commercial growing in this region.

The strength of orchid growing today is due to many pioneers, but three men in particular deserve mention as founding fathers of orchid growing in Singapore. They are John Laycock, Emile Galistan, and R. E. Holttum. Laycock and Galistan were private growers, while Holttum was the Director of the Singapore Botanic Gardens during the 1930s. According to Holttum, writing in the *Malayan Orchid Review* for 1988, John Laycock actually founded the society, calling Galistan and others together for the purpose. Holttum's contribution was subsequent to this, but his impact was enormous. The results of his research, applying the then newly discovered methods of sterile culture of orchid seeds, laid the foundation for today's cut-flower industry as well as for the range of plants available to private growers.

Professor Holttum's constant encouragement and promotion of orchid horticulture continued to his 95th year. Shortly before his death, he kindly consented to write the foreword for this book. In a very real sense, we today stand on the shoulders of Laycock, Galistan, Holttum, and many other pioneers and later enthusiasts, and this book is affectionately and gratefully dedicated to the memory of them all.

Foreword by R. E. Holttum

When I went to Singapore in 1922, I knew nothing about methods for cultivation of orchids, and they were not an important feature in the Botanic Gardens. I gradually discovered that no-one was giving any critical thought to the subject, and that such thought was necessary to improve our practice.

Most tropical orchids are epiphytes. Their roots are exposed to the air and evidently need such exposure for development and for carrying out their vital functions in the growth of orchid plants. This fact presents the basic problem to cultivators: how to keep the roots active while keeping the plants in containers which are easily handled and moved. The first considerable experiments in orchid culture in pots were made by growers in Europe, where the plants had to be kept in greenhouses. The open air environment of orchid culture in tropical lowlands is quite different.

The object of this book is to record effective methods which have been gradually developed by successful growers, as well as the accessory skills needed to promote the best possible growth and flowering. Orchids are now of major importance in tropical gardens. They are also often grown on balconies and similar places. Here for the first time is an attempt to bring together all information about handling them. It is an important development in tropical horticulture, and I am very glad to welcome it.

Chapter One

Describing and Identifying Orchids

The orchid family is a very varied one. Orchid flowers come in many sizes, shapes and colours, and the plants themselves are almost equally diverse. Some grow on trees, some on rocks, others on the ground, and some are climbers. The great majority of cultivated orchids are not found in the wild, but are hybrids created by human beings. Even though this book deals only with orchids that grow in tropical conditions, this diversity means that there is no single way to grow them. Rather, the key to good orchid growing is to be able to adjust the growing conditions to the needs of particular plants. An essential first step is therefore to identify the plants. Having identified them, the conditions necessary for good growing can be provided. This is a matter of knowing how much light, air and water the plants need, and what sort of potting or bedding materials are suitable.

Because orchids are so varied, it is necessary to be clear about the ways in which they differ. This chapter helps us to understand some of the terms used to describe orchids, and Chapter Two describes the common types of cultivated orchid. Chapter Three deals with the main principles of cultivation, and describes different cultivation regimes. Each regime is a set of conditions suitable for a particular range of orchids.

Opposite: This is an orchid, but what orchid is it? Finding out what it is, or better still its name, is the first step to growing the orchid you have acquired. This one is called *Dendrobium* Dora Poong.

FORM OF THE PLANT: MONOPODIAL OR SYMPODIAL?

Monopodial Orchids
A basic distinction is between monopodial and sympodial orchids. Monopodial orchids are those in which the stem (or stems) grows indefinitely. New leaves always grow from the end of a stem. Usually the stem grows upright, and the plants are often climbers if the stem is a long one. In the natural state, many climbing orchids obtain support by putting out roots along their stems. These aerial roots, as they are called, attach themselves to any surface they meet. Very extensive root systems can be found in undisturbed, mature

plants. Unattended or wild plants can reach a considerable height if they are also climbers, and will sprawl over if adequate support is not provided. Other monopodial orchids have very short stems, and may lack aerial roots. These are not climbers.

Sometimes the plants may produce side shoots lower down the stem, forming a clump of stems, but in most cases they grow for years as a single stem. This single stem with indefinite growth is the main characteristic of the monopodial group. Once the plant is full-grown, the stem tends to be the same thickness throughout, and the leaves are all about the same size, The flower spike (or inflorescence) grows from the side of the stem, not from the end (the crown).

Sympodial Orchids

The majority of tropical orchids are not monopodial. They are sympodial and have a pattern of growth in which there is a succession of shoots or bulb-like stems (called pseudobulbs), each growing from the base of the one before. Each pseudobulb only grows for a limited time and then stops. These shoots or pseudobulbs come in various forms.

Top: A typical monopodial orchid. The stem grows straight up, and the flowers are on spikes growing from the side of the stem.

Left: A typical sympodial orchid. This one is at a show. The plant consists of a little clump of pseudobulbs, each of which has grown from the base of an earlier one. The flowers are on a spike at the end of one of them. Other sympodials might have more leaves, or no bulbs, or the flowers might come from another part of the plant, but they all share the same way of growing, namely a succession of pseudobulbs or shoots.

Sometimes the stem is so sheathed in leaves that it cannot be seen at all. In other cases the stem is visible as a bulb or stem, that can be short or long, smooth or wrinkled, with many leaves or only one. Often the pseudobulbs are close together, but in some orchids they are spaced out along a rhizome, which is a kind of creeping stem.

The flower spike of a sympodial orchid may arise from the very end of the pseudobulb, from some point along it, from the base of the pseudobulb, or even from the rhizome, as the case may be. The roots are found at the base of each pseudobulb or along the rhizome, though sometimes a young plant complete with roots may develop from a bud high up on the parent stem. Although the sympodial orchids include plants that may look very different, what distinguishes them all is the fact that they have successive pseudobulbs of limited growth.

MANNER OF GROWTH: TERRESTRIAL, EPIPHYTIC, CLIMBING OR LITHOPHYTIC?

As well as establishing whether an unknown orchid is monopodial or sympodial, it is also helpful to know if it is terrestrial, epiphytic, climbing or lithophytic. That is, does it normally grow on the ground, on trees, up a support, or on rocks?

Terrestrial Orchids
These orchids have the following characteristics.
• They grow and flower on the ground.
• They are best grown in well drained soil or peat-based potting mixtures.
• They are a relatively small group in tropical lowland cultivation.

Epiphytic Orchids
These are the main group of tropical orchids.
• They grow naturally on trees. They are not parasites. They do not take any nourishment from the trees they grow on, but only use them as supports.
• They have roots that often grow on the surface of pots or potting material, exposed to the elements.
• They need potting with a very open and free-draining material that is not soil.

Epiphytic orchids are commonly grown in pieces of brick or charcoal, styrofoam pellets, fern root or coconut fibre. These materials retain moisture

Below: *Phaius tankervilleae*. This terrestrial species occurs in lowland and lower level mountain jungle throughout South East Asia.

but allow aeration, and are more or less long-lasting. They can also be grown in wooden baskets, on fern root slabs, on logs or tree stumps, or in any way that mimics nature and provides anchorage for roots. The roots grow over and into any support or potting material. Epiphytic orchids are never half-buried under the potting mixture, rather they sit right on top of it.

Climbing Orchids
These orchids are easily recognized.
• They often originate on the ground, but climb up trees or bushes.
• They have aerial roots that cling to any suitable support.
• They need a better draining compost than terrestrials. Some can be treated as epiphytes.

Climbing orchids are always monopodial, and are usually grown in pots or beds with wooden posts to which the aerial roots attach themselves. They need a good deal of space. Some types can reach a height of several metres and are therefore not easily moved. As a result, although important for the cut-flower industry, they are now less common in private collections than in times when space was less precious.

Opposite Top: *Vanda sanderiana.* This is one of the most spectacular of epiphytic orchid species, native to the Philippines. The orchids grow on the tree, but they are not parasites.

Opposite Bottom: Climbing orchids. This shows the appearance of a well cultivated bed of climbing hybrids. The plants are supported by posts and rails hidden in the mass of leaves and aerial roots. They are growing in full sun, which encourages flowering.

Above: *Bulbophyllum membranaceum.* Photographed growing wild in Singapore, this inconspicuous little orchid is clearly flourishing on its granite outcrop. Lithophytic orchids are generally treated as epiphytes in cultivation.

Lithophytic Orchids
These orchids are fairly rare.
• They grow on rocks.
• They need a well drained compost.

These orchids grow with their roots exploring the cracks and crevices of suitable rocky surfaces, so that even when the rock is in a sunny place, the roots are protected from excessive drying out. They are not very common in cultivation and are usually treated as epiphytes or as terrestrials with very free-draining compost.

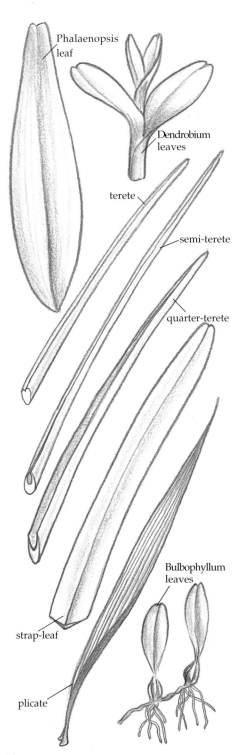

Phalaenopsis leaf

Dendrobium leaves

terete

semi-terete

quarter-terete

Bulbophyllum leaves

strap-leaf

plicate

HOW PLANTS DIFFER

Even within the broad divisions of monopodial or sympodial growth, orchids differ greatly as plants, that is, in their vegetative structures. These differences reflect adaptation to a diversity of habitats. Since orchids are often not in flower, these differences are helpful in identifying them.

Orchid Leaves

Orchids have what botanists call simple leaves, that is the leaves are not made up of lobes or leaflets. Some plants have leaves that are plicate, that is they are thin with many lengthwise pleats. Most plants have leaves that are thicker, smooth and V-shaped in cross-section. Such leaves are called conduplicate. A number of orchids have long, thin, terete (cylindrical) leaves, which may be grooved. Orchids that have elongated stems or pseudobulbs covered in leaves almost always have the leaves in two rows alternately along the length of the stem or pseudobulb.

Many conduplicate leaves are thick and fleshy. This can give the impression that the orchids would be able to withstand drought well, like cacti, but this is not usually so for tropical orchids. Orchids from regions with periodic dry spells can withstand drought, but this is usually because they have succulent pseudobulbs rather than succulent leaves. Such orchids lose their leaves seasonally and are difficult to grow and flower well in the tropics unless they are dried out for a few months each year. Tropical lowland orchids usually grow all year round.

Left: Different types of orchid leaves.

Shedding Leaves

Some orchids are seasonal. They flower only at certain times of the year, and often they lose all their leaves, making fresh growth annually. However, most tropical lowland orchids are not very seasonal, due to the more uniform climate in which they grow.

Orchids that are not strongly seasonal are evergreen, and only shed their leaves erratically and gradually. The bare pseudobulbs or stems that are left are usually also green, and contain stores of food and water. Especially in sympodial orchids, new shoots, roots or flower sprays may start from such old stems. Therefore it is not usual to prune or cut back bare stems or pseudobulbs, since it is often the case that they are the basis for flowering and further growth. Even with non-seasonal orchids, such as are mostly grown in the lowland tropics, it is also the case that older, apparently barren pseudobulbs may bear further flowers or shoots if left to do so.

In general, monopodial orchids are less apt to shed their leaves completely or to be strongly seasonal than sympodials. Flowering, on the other hand, can be seasonal, triggered by variations in light (day-length), night time temperature, or humidity. Even those seasonal monopodials such as Rhynchostylis, which need quite dry periods in order to induce flowering, do not shed all their leaves. While it is often easy to grow sympodial orchids starting with a few leafless pseudobulbs and no roots, it is usually necessary with monopodial orchids to have intact roots and leaves and for the plant not to be excessively dessicated. For this reason, the first attempts to import tropical orchids into the West met with greater success where seasonal sympodials were concerned. Monopodial orchids were generally rarer in those early collections.

Above: *Dendrobium hercoglossum.* This attractive Thai species prefers a seasonal climate. It sheds its leaves, and flowers on the old bare pseudobulbs. Many Dendrobium hybrids also flower on older pseudobulbs. These should therefore not be pruned.

When terete-leaved orchids are crossed with others with strap leaves, the offspring tend to have leaves of intermediate form, that is, long and rather succulent, but with a deep channel in the upper surface. Such leaves are known as semi-terete. Similarly, further crossing with flat-leaved parents dilutes the terete effect further, and one obtains broadly channelled succulent leaves, and these are known, quite logically, as quarter-terete plants.

Roots

The roots of epiphytic and climbing orchids are one of their most striking characteristics. Most common garden plants have a single central tap root that goes straight down, and numerous smaller roots. All these roots taper down to a fine network of quite tiny roots, covered in root-hairs. Orchid roots, on the other hand, like palm and bamboo roots, are roughly the same diameter throughout their length; there is no tap root. Where the roots are exposed to the air, they are covered in a silvery grey coat, the velamen, which darkens with age. It is absorbent and rather spongy. The root tip is usually green, and, like the leaves, can photosynthesize, i.e. build up sugar

Top: A Phalaenopsis plant growing on a slab of artificial fern root. The roots support the plant by clinging to the slab. The roots are a silvery-grey colour, and do not taper but are the same width as they grow. In a wild plant such roots will spread for many metres along tree branches.

Left: A Dendrobium plant lifted out of its pot, showing the mass of roots winding round and round inside the pot. The potting material has to leave enough space for this. Dendrobiums like to have rather crowded roots.

from light, carbon dioxide and water using chlorophyll. Where a root comes into contact with a suitable surface, such as a branch, it grows into close contact with it and sticks, and cannot be pulled away without damage.

When such roots cease to be exposed, because they have grown under bark or into compost or potting materials, they become pale and swollen. They do not show the many roothairs characteristic of ordinary plants, and they easily rot if they get waterlogged. Terrestrial and lithophytic orchids more often have hairy roots, and are more tolerant of damp conditions; but even in these cases, good drainage is the rule rather than the exception.

Roots are essential anchors for epiphytic orchids, which often grow high above ground, sometimes in quite exposed and windy positions. The grip of the roots is a very strong one. Even dead roots show considerable strength in some species, and still help secure the plant. Moreover the roots spread very widely over the available surfaces: it is not uncommon for roots to run several metres along a branch. Because of this tendency, moving a plant grown on a bench usually involves cutting or pulling away the roots anchoring the pot to the bench. This is one reason for not moving the plants too often.

Top: A mass of aerial roots in a bed of climbing orchids, *Vanda* Miss Joaquim. The roots will stick to any suitable surface they encounter, thus helping support the plants.

Right: *Chiloschista usneoides*. This epiphytic species has no green leaves at all. Its roots both absorb water and manufacture carbohydrates by photosynthesis, like the leaves of other orchids.

17

Orchid Flowers

Flowers from different orchid plants may look very different, but they all have the same basic structure of three petals and three sepals. Petals and sepals together are collectively called tepals. The petals and sepals alternate around the centre of the flower, where there is a central structure called the column. The column contains both the female and male reproductive organs, namely the stigma, a hollow sticky pad that receives the pollen, and the anther, which contains the pollen.

In most cultivated orchids the anther, which is at the end of the column, is covered by a little cap, the anther cap. Under it the pollen is found as two or more masses or pollen bodies, called pollinia, which tend to stick to anything that removes the anther cap. The whole of the pollen is thus transferred from one orchid flower to another when cross-pollination takes place. This ensures very large numbers of seeds are formed.

A representative orchid flower, in this case *Aranda* Christine, is shown. At the top and standing straight up is a sepal. Then there are two petals, one on either side, followed by the other two sepals, also one on either side but lower down. These two lower sepals are called lateral sepals. They may be a different shape from the top sepal, as in the example shown. Below and opposite the top sepal, is a modified petal called the lip. The lip is below the column, or enclosing it. Some orchids, such as *Aranda* Christine, have rather small lips, but many others have large or highly coloured lips. In the wild, the lip helps attract insects to land on it as part of the means whereby the flowers are pollinated, but in cultivated orchids the colour and shape of the lip reflect the efforts of breeders and it has mostly lost its natural function. Nevertheless, insects do sometimes land on the lips of cultivated hybrids, where they may carry off the pollen and thus cause the flowers to wilt.

The flowers are carried on spikes (inflorescences). A spike may be erect (upright), arched,

Above: *Aranda* Christine. A number of 'Christines' have been a success in the cut-flower trade and among growers, in particular Nos. 1, 27, 72, 80, 1005 and 1009.

Opposite: The different flower parts of an *Aranda* Christine.

or pendulous (hanging down). A spike may arise from the end of a stem or pseudobulb, or from some point along the stem or pseudobulb, in which case the spike is said to be lateral. When a lateral flower spike starts to grow, it starts as a bud opposite the base of a leaf (an axillary bud). In some orchids (such as Oncidiums) the spike arises from the base of the pseudobulb.

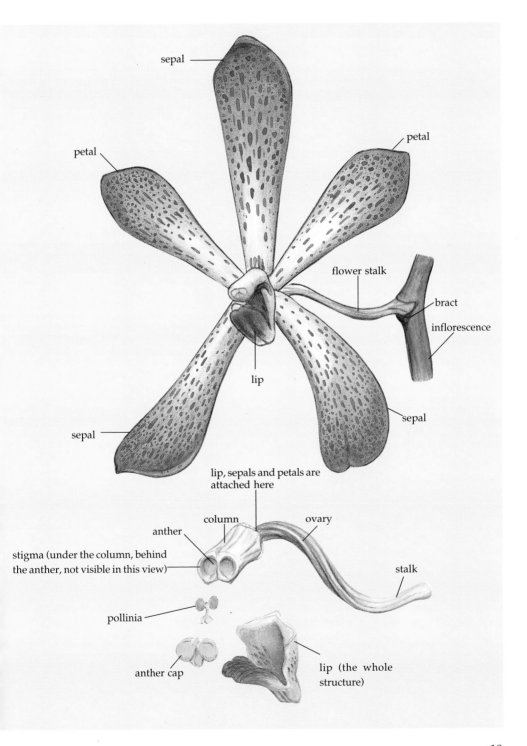

sepal

petal

petal

flower stalk

bract

inflorescence

lip

sepal

sepal

lip, sepals and petals are
attached here

column

ovary

anther

stalk

stigma (under the column, behind
the anther, not visible in this view)

pollinia

anther cap

lip (the whole
structure)

Species and Hybrids

Most of the orchids in cultivation today are not wild plants (species), but are hybrids. Most hybrids are man-made, though some occur in nature. Primary hybrids are crossings between different parent species, and they may be further crossed with other hybrids or species over many generations. Orchids hybridize very freely, and many thousands of man-made hybrids have been produced since 1853 when the first one was produced in England by John Dominy. Fortunately, a record has been kept of the parentage of virtually all these hybrids, and it is therefore usually possible, given the name of an orchid, to trace its parentage back to the original parent species. For this reason, orchid enthusiasts usually only grow plants of known parentage, especially if they themselves are interested in creating hybrids.

ORCHID NAMES

Genus and Species Names

Every orchid has two parts in its name. Take, for example, *Oncidium sphacelatum*: the first name tells us that this is a plant in the genus Oncidium. There are many different Oncidiums, and the second name, *sphacelatum*, tells us which of the 500 or so different kinds of Oncidium this one is. Because this example is a species (a plant existing naturally in the wild), the species name does not have a capital letter.

Genus and species names are italicized when referring to a particular species. The genus name is often abbreviated: for example, Onc. is used for Oncidium. Latin is used for the names as it was originally the language of learning in Western Europe, and it is retained by international convention. Sometimes the names used by botanists are not the same as those used in horticulture and hybrid registration. In this book horticultural names are usually given.

Sometimes a species has one or more recognized varieties. The varietal names are also italicized. For example, *Arachnis flos-aeris* has two varieties; the deep maroon var *insignis*, and the patterned var *gracilis*. The contraction 'var' is not italicized.

Hybrid Names

A hybrid, called a grex by botanists, also has a two-part name. Take for example the common *Oncidium* Goldiana, often wrongly called *Oncidium* Golden Shower. This is a hybrid between two species, *Onc. flexuosum* and *Onc. sphacelatum*. It is still an Oncidium, but instead of the species name, we have the hybrid name, Goldiana, which is given a capital letter and is not italicized. Latin is not used for hybrid names.

In order to name a hybrid, it has to be registered with the Royal Horticultural Society, London. Names cannot exceed three words, or duplicate a name already used for that genus. For further details see page 190. The RHS maintains lists of all hybrids ever registered, called Sander's Lists. These lists, recently computerized, allow the owner of a named orchid to trace its parentage back to the original species. Therefore, enthusiasts avoid unnamed plants, since they can never be used as parents of any future registered hybrid.

An Orchid Family Tree

Arachnis hookeriana var *luteola*

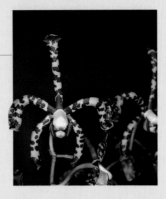

Arachnis flos-aeris var *gracilis*

Arachnis Maggie Oei

Vanda insignis

Aranda Majula 'Rimau' AM/OSSEA

The pale 'luteola' form of *Arach. hookeriana* crossed with *Arach. flos-aeris* var *gracilis* gave the patterning that made the offspring, *Arach.* Maggie Oei, a popular cut flower for many years after it arrived on the scene in 1940. Maggie Oei in turn served as a parent, being crossed with *Vanda insignis* to give *Aranda* Majula. The Vanda parent contributed to the deeper coloration and heavy texture of Majula, but the Arachnis influence stayed strong in the shape of the flower. It has always proved difficult to turn the scorpion form into one with broader tepals, since the shape is rather dominant, and most Arandas are sterile and cannot themselves be used as parents.

Names for Man-made Genera

The plural of genus is genera. When two orchids from different genera are crossed, a new genus is created and a new generic name has to be invented. An example is *Aranda* Christine. The name 'Aranda' is a sort of mixed name created by combining Arachnis and Vanda. Such hybrids are called bi-generic or inter-generic. Sander's Lists tell us Christine has the parents *Arachnis hookeriana* and *Vanda* Hilo Blue. We can see from this that *Arach. hookeriana* is a species and *V.* Hilo Blue is a hybrid from a different genus.

Up to three genus names can be combined in this way, for example Brassolaeliocattleya (abbreviated Blc.) is a combination of Brassavola, Laelia and Cattleya. Most hybrids with three or more genera in the parentage ('multigenerics') have a genus name created by adding the suffix '-ara' to the name of a person to be honoured instead. 'Holttumara' is thus a generic name for plants with Arachnis, Vanda and Renanthera in the parentage.

A third term is sometimes added to a name, for example *Aranda* Hilda Galistan 'Suntan'. This third term is called the cultivar epithet. This is a name given when a plant has received an award by a recognized orchid society. The awarded plant and its subsequent cuttings or divisions form a recognized variety, or cultivar. Awards consists of First Class Certificate (FCC), Award of Merit (AM) and High Commendation Certificate (HCC).

Top: *Kagawara* Christie Low. This is a multigeneric (Ascocentrum x Renanthera x Vanda).

Left: *Aranda* Hilda Galistan.

Professor Eric Holttum (1895–1990)

The first Holttumara was *Holttumara* Cochineal, recorded in the *Malayan Orchid Review* for 1958, the parentage being *Aranda* Hilda Galistan 'Suntan' x *Renanthera coccinea*. Another early Holttumara was *Holtt.* Loke Tuck Yip, shown below. The name honours Professor Eric Holttum for his pioneering work in orchid breeding while Director of the Singapore Botanic Gardens from 1925 to 1949.

Professor Holttum, who was also a founder member of the Malayan Orchid Society (now the

Right: Professor Holttum, photographed in the herbarium at the Singapore Botanic Gardens.

Below: *Holttumara* Loke Tuck Yip (*Aranda* Lucy Laycock x *Renanthera storiei*).

Orchid Society of South East Asia, OSSEA), was the first in Singapore to try propagating orchids from seeds in glass flasks on an artificial culture medium. At the time it was a revolutionary technique, developed originally by Knudson, though now universally used. Professor Holttum also did much to promote gardening generally, and he was well known for his interest in the local methods of cultivation already in use in Singapore by market gardeners and horticulturists in the first half of the century. Most unusually, the wartime Japanese administration permitted Holttum to work, and he commented that, "It was only during the Japanese occupation that I was able to devote my whole time over considerable periods to taxonomic study, and I learned a great deal in three-and-a-half years. This was really my preparation for the work I have tried to undertake since my retirement from Singapore in 1954." ['Retrospective on a 90th Birthday', *Kew Bulletin*, Vol. 41 (3) (1986)]. Professor Holttum was indeed to accomplish a further 35 years of work in taxonomy before finally having to stop through ill health in his ninety-fourth year.

Chapter Two

Common Cultivated Groups

This chapter gives a very brief description of typical orchids in the various cultivated genera, so that the owner of an unidentified plant will have some idea of what it is likely to be, and hence how to treat it. The kind of cultural regime required is mentioned, but more details of cultivation in general and for specific groups are given in Chapters Three and Four respectively.

MONOPODIAL ORCHIDS

A General Note
Monopodial orchids have been very extensively hybridized. Almost any form of plant intermediate between tall climbers and short stemmed epiphytes can be found, and the distinctions are to some extent arbitrary.

The rule of thumb is that the shorter the plant and the broader the leaves, the more shade and water are needed. Tall plants almost always require full or high sunlight to do well. Shorter ones are more variable. There is no substitute for experience in such matters. Although the details that follow are intended to help identify orchid groups for the reader, individual plants often have individual requirements, and a rule of thumb is simply a basis for deciding what to do when more definite information is lacking.

CLIMBING ORCHIDS

Arachnis and Related Genera (Scorpion or Spider Orchids)
(including some Aranda, Renanthera, Renantanda, Kagawara, Aeridachnis, Aeridovanda, Arachnostylis, Holttumara, and Renanopsis.)

These plants have relatively flat strap-like leaves in two rows, and stems up to two cm diameter, usually less. Aerial roots are produced at intervals on the stem. The flower sprays are usually long, the flowers rarely having very wide tepals, and tending to show the 'scorpion' or 'spider' shape of Arachnis. Plants range in size and height, but many are tall, flowering at over 2 m.
Regime
These are full sun climbing or bench orchids depending on their size and the height at which they will flower. They usually need posts for support.

Vanda (Terete and Semi-terete)
These climbing plants have upright slim stems less than one cm diameter.

Left: *Renanopsis* Lena Rowold (*Renanthera storiei* x *Vandopsis lissochiloides*). An example of the Renanthera influence in colour and form. The other parent, Vandopsis, gives size to the plant and a heavy texture to the flowers.

Centre Left: *Aranda* Myrna Braga. This early Aranda (1956) also shows the Scorpion Orchid form strongly. The parentage is *Arachnis* Ishbel x *Vanda merrillii*.

Opposite Centre: *Arachnis* Ishbel. It is easy to see why Arachnis plants — Spider Orchids — were so named. The word 'Arachnis' comes from the Greek and means 'spider-like'. In fact, Arachnis orchids are usually known as 'Scorpion Orchids'. This early Arachnis cross, registered in 1940, shows the typical 'spider' or 'scorpion' shape of Arachnis flowers.

Below: *Aranthera* Beatrice Ng. This plant, a cross registered in 1961 between *Renanthera storiei* and *Arachnis* Ishbel, shows the typical form of a climbing strap-leaved climber. The flowers, unusually for a Renanthera cross, are yellow rather than red or orange, but the form of the flower is closer to the Renanthera parent.

Right: *Mokara* Chark Kuan (*Aranda* Christine x *Ascocenda* Cholburi). Still showing the influence of the Arachnis parentage in its shape, this multigeneric hybrid shows the improved size and shape of flowers sought after by breeders.

Bottom: A Renanthera hybrid. The brilliant red colour of most Renanthera species and hybrids has long made them a favourite with growers and hybridizers. They make their impact through the masses of flowers on the spreading flower spray. The individual flowers have a characteristic shape well shown in this photograph.

27

The leaves are either cylindrical (terete) and well spaced out along the stem, or with a single deep channel (semi-terete), closer on the stem, in two rows. The stem bears aerial roots at intervals. Flowers are on lateral spikes, not from the end of the stem.

Regime

These are full sun climbers, best grown in beds with post supports. The greater the spacing out of leaves along the stem, the more the plant will need a support.

Top Left: *Kagawara* Neo. Kagawaras have Vanda, Ascocentrum and Renanthera in their parentage. The flower shape and red colour of Renanthera still shows through in the offspring, but the flatter broader Vanda shape is also contributing. Ascocentrums usually have a miniaturizing effect.

Bottom Left: *Renantanda* Soh Kim Kang. The Renanthera and Vanda influences are nicely blended in this 1982 hybrid (*Renanthera storiei* x *Vanda* Dawn Nishimura).

Opposite Top: *Vanda* Miss Joaquim. This hybrid (*V. hookeriana* x *V. teres*) was discovered by Agnes Joaquim in her Singapore garden in 1893. In the years before World War II it was a staple garden plant in Singapore, Malaya and later Hawaii, where it was important in the cut-flower trade. It is far more free-flowering and easy-growing than either of the parent species.

Opposite Left: *Ascocenda* Mani Beauty (*Ascda.* Yip Sum Wah x *Vanda* Miss Joaquim). Most Ascocendas are not made with terete-leaved Vandas, but this one is. Consequently it has semi-terete leaves and flowers showing the Joaquim influence.

Opposite Right: *Vanda* Norbert Alphonso. Registered in 1950, this was one of the many terete-leaved and semi-terete hybrids stimulated by the success of *V.* Miss Joaquim. The parents are *V.* Alice Laycock, and *V.* Cooperi. Such hybrids have a characteristic flower form with horizontally twisted lateral petals, and have predominatly mauve shades.

Vandaceous Quarter-terete Hybrids (including some Vanda, Ascocenda, Renantanda, Bokchoonara, Vandaenopsis, Laycockara and Trevorara). The leaves are more or less succulent, long, narrow and channelled, sometimes requiring support, sometimes capable of growing and flowering without support; the plants are more stout and robust than the terete or semi-terete Vandas.

Leaves are in two rows, with aerial roots at intervals up the stem. Flowers are from lateral spikes, not from the end of the stem.

Top Left: *Vandaenopsis* David Marshall. The terete-leaved Paraphalaenopsis parent has given this semi-terete hybrid long deeply grooved leaves.

Bottom Left: *Vanda* Reverend Masao Yamada. This quarter-terete Vanda was produced in 1983.

Below: *Vandaenopsis* Laycock Child. Another example where *Paraphalaenopsis laycockii* has passed on its influence. The shape and colour of the flower also owe much to this parent. The plant is short, not a climber, and this too is from the Paraphalaenopsis parent.

Regime
These are full sun bench orchids. Some may flower well in less than full sun. Support may be needed in the form of a post in the pot.

EPIPHYTIC ORCHIDS
Plants in this group may be climbers also, but they are epiphytic. The stems may be too short to need a support, or they may even hang down. However, as long as we are considering monopodial orchids, we know that the stems will go on producing new leaves.

Ascocentrum, Miniature Ascocenda
These are miniature strap-leaved plants like miniature Vandas. The leaves may be succulent. Larger Ascocendas are also available. These are treated like strap-leaved or quarter-terete Vandas.
Regime
These are light shade hanging orchids. The plants are best hung in baskets or perforated pots with a regime of ample watering.

Top Right: *Vanda* T. M. A. This peach-tinted quarter-terete Vanda is characteristic of many similar hybrids from South East Asia.

Centre Right: *Ascocentrum curvifolium*. Ascocentrums are small plants with brightly coloured flowers in dense sprays. A specimen plant like the one shown makes a striking sight in full flower. Ascocentrums have been extensively hybridized with Vandas to give a range of miniature Vanda-like plants called Ascocendas.

Right: *Bokchoonara* Khaw Bian Huat. The grooved leaves show the influence of the terete Paraphalaenopsis strain in this multigeneric hybrid. The parents are *Arachnopsis* Eric Holttum x *Ascocenda* Tan Chai Beng. This orchid is grown as a Vandaceous quarter-terete.

Paraphalaenopsis and Related Hybrids

The leaves are long (up to 60 cm) and terete (cylindrical) or almost terete, and apt to hang down. They point in all directions. The stems are short. The flowers are on rather short sprays from the lower part of the stem.

Regime

Shade or light shade is needed, with ample water. The plants are best hung leaves downward to make them more manageable, otherwise pots on benches can be used.

Phalaenopsis, Doritis, Doritaenopsis (Moth or Moon Orchids)

These plants have a few large broad fleshy leaves on either side of the short stem. Usually there are fewer than ten pairs of leaves. In large plants the leaves may hang down, especially if the plant is grown horizontally. Flower sprays are usually long, with a few star-shaped flowers or more numerous broad rounded flowers in rows, usually white or pink, which are sometimes striped or spotted.

Opposite Left: *Phalaenopsis* Mouchette. These orchids are becoming increasingly varied in colour, but the ideal shape remains flat and circular.

Opposite Right: *Phalaenopsis* Kathleen Ai. Candy striped Phalaenopsis are beautiful but no longer novel. The parents of this one are *Phal.* Waimanalo Sunrise x *Phal.* Wendel George.

Opposite Bottom: *Renanthopsis* Margaret. The Renanthera parentage gives an orange hue, and a taller plant, but the flowers are more like Paraphalaenopsis in shape.

Right: A Phalaenopsis hybrid (*Phal.* Shogun x *Phal.* Spitzberg). Evocative names in the parents, but the offspring is yet to be named.

Regime

These are shade or light shade epiphytes needing plenty of moisture but good ventilation. The pots can be tipped up to allow the leaves to hang down (except Doritis). If well watered, the plants do well on rafts.

Below: *Paraphalaenopsis denevei.* This plant is growing upright in its pot, but the plants do just as well grown upside down on a slab of fern root.

Above: *Doritaenopsis* Elizabeth Waldheim. Created from *Doritis pulcherrima* x *Phalaenopsis* Lam Soon, this hybrid shows the upright deep mauve spike typical of Doritis.

Top Left: *Phalaenopsis violacea* (Borneo variety). A fine example of this beautiful and popular species. The flowers have a spicy fragrance.

Left: The blue colour and tesselated pattern are typical of the blue Vanda, *Vanda coerulea*, and its hybrids.

Vandaceous (Strap-leaved)

(including Vanda, Vandopsis, Rhynchostylis, Aerides, and intergenerics from these, also some Ascocenda) These mostly large and robust plants have large curved strap-like leaves, close together in two rows on the stem. The roots are thick. Flowers are often relatively flat and large, often scented.

Regime

These are shade epiphytes, though Aerides and Ascocenda tolerate more sun. They are best grown in a very coarse potting medium or in baskets without additional material. Frequent watering and a humid environment are needed. The plants generally do better hanging.

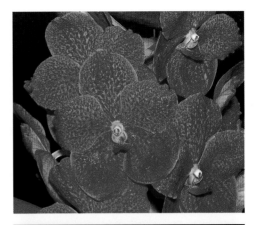

Top Right: This striking hybrid is typical of the many large-flowered Vandas bred in Thailand especially. The large size and flat, round form of the flowers is due to the *Vanda sanderiana* parentage.

Centre Right: *Asconopsis* Irene Dobkin is one of the earliest (1968) and best known crosses of this type. *Phalaenopsis* Doris x *Ascocentrum miniatum* is a white Phalaenopsis blended with an orange miniature, and the result is a striking colour in a Phalaenopsis type flower. Such innovative crosses are being seen more and more often.

Below: *Vanda insignis*. This species is one of many with smaller flowers than the usual hybrid strap-leaved Vandas, but with an undeniable charm. Most of the strap-leaved Vanda species — though not the larger hybrids — are very pleasantly scented.

35

Left: *Aerides lawrenceae*. This photograph shows the strap-leaved style of growth. Aerides plants have sprays of numerous flowers with a horn-shaped lip. This species is prized for its scent and the relatively large size of its flowers.

Below: *Rhynchostylis gigantea*. Rhynchostylis orchids are known as Foxtail Orchids, on account of their arching sprays of densely packed flowers.

Bottom: *Christieara* Ramiah. A cross that combines the size and shape of Ascocenda with the numerous flowers of Aerides.

SYMPODIAL ORCHIDS

EPIPHYTIC ORCHIDS
Cattleya Alliance
(including Cattleya, Brassavola, Laelia, Sophronitis, Encyclia, Epidendrum and crosses involving these and other related genera).

These plants have upright pseudobulbs that swell towards the upper end, with one or two leaves only. The leaves are often stiff and leathery. The flower spike is always from the end of the pseudobulb. There may be a few large showy flowers or a larger number of smaller flowers. The flowers usually have a more or less ornate and conspicuous lip.

Regime
These plants need light shade and well drained potting mixtures. They grow well if they are not repotted too frequently.

Top Right: A Cattleya alliance flower. These are often large showy orchids, usually fragrant. The Cattleya alliance orchids come from the New World (tropical and subtropical America). They are very popular in temperate regions as hothouse plants.

Second Right: Another Cattleya alliance hybrid. Note the small number of flowers on the spray, which is usual in plants in this group. The large striking lip is typical.

Third Right: *Epicattleya* Fireball. A larger number of flowers is common in Epicattleyas, as are the narrower sepals and petals and the contrasting lip.

Bottom Right: This is a 'minicat', *Laeliocattleya* Long Tone (*Lc.* Netrasiri Doll x *C.* Thospol Spot). The trend to miniaturization has led to many beautiful hybrids with compact deeply coloured flower sprays like this one. Miniature Cattleya alliance plants are often favourites with balcony growers as they are usually quite hardy.

Dendrobium

These plants typically have upright pseudobulbs with leaves in two rows. The pseudobulbs are usually swollen at the very base, and in the middle part. The leaves on the lower part of the pseudobulbs are small or absent. Flower spikes arise from the end of the pseudobulb or from lateral buds, and are often long and arching. However, Dendrobiums are quite variable, some have pendulous stems, others short pseudobulbs with few leaves. Some

Left: *Brassavola fragrans*. Much used in hybridizing for its lip, this easily grown species is also kept for its own sake. The terete leaves are unusual in the Cattleya alliance.

Below: *Dendrobium* Bobby Mesina x *Dendrobium* Shogun. This hybrid is unregistered, so can only be identified by its parentage. Dendrobiums of this form are known as 'intermediate type', since they are intermediate between the Phalaenopsis and antelope forms.

may flower on short sprays along the length of the pseudobulb. Many common cut flowers are Dendrobiums, especially in white, mauve and yellow.
Regime
Light shade Dendrobiums with upright canes, the 'antelope' Dendrobiums, can be hardened to grow in full sun. Water well when new shoots appear and again during growth, give less when the lower part of the plant is resting.

Top Right: A flowering Dendrobium. Dendrobiums are among the commonest cultivated orchids in the lowland tropics, and after the spider orchids are perhaps the most typical of OSSEA hybrids. Many are easy to grow, free-flowering, and suitable for the cut-flower trade. This type is called an 'antelope' Dendrobium from the pair of erect 'horns' formed from the petals of each flower.

Right: *Dendrobium* Lay Keng: mauve is the commonest colour for Dendrobiums.

Below: *Dendrobium* Jayapura (*Den.* Lily Doo x *Den. superbum*). Contrasting lips are a feature of many Dendrobiums.

Above: *Dendrobium* Alkaff Lion City. Another intermediate hybrid, but much nearer the Phalaenopsis form. This one nicely shows the elegance of a well arched spray. Obtaining a long spray free of blemishes from pests in every flower is not easy.

Top Left: *Dendrobium anosmum.* Also known as *Dendrobium superbum*, this species has a most unsuitable name. '*Anosmum*' is Latin for 'without scent'; but these flowers have a strong and rather sweet scent somewhat like raspberries or strawberries. The pseudobulbs hang down, and flower only after they have shed their leaves.

Left: *Dendrobium* Lady Hochoy. This hybrid is typical of the 'antelope' Dendrobiums, so called because the twisted petals look like antelope horns. The plants are often large, though miniatures are coming in, and flower freely, usually on the older back bulbs. Dendrobiums like this are native to New Guinea, and have also been widely hybridized in Singapore and Malaysia.

Oncidium (Soft-leaved)

The pseudobulbs are oval and flattened. The leaves are thin and grass-like, longest from the top of the pseudobulb. Flower spikes are from the base of the pseudobulbs, usually long with many small flowers (up to three cm across). The leaves may obscure the pseudobulbs. Plants may be miniature (about 15 cm high) or larger (to about 40 cm). Flowers have a distinctive lip, very large and flat compared to the rest of the tepals.

Regime

Light shade is needed. The roots are thin relative to the size of the plants, and potting media therefore need to be correspondingly finer. However, the plants do not like to be too wet, and need good drainage.

Oncidium (Mule-eared)

The plants have one or a few large leathery leaves (to about 30 cm) per shoot. The stem is not visible as it is covered by sheaths. The leaf is usually dull greyish green and may have some speckling. The flower spikes come from the base of the shoot, and the flowers are larger and fewer than in the soft-leaved Oncidiums.

Regime

Light shade is needed. Do not water excessively.

Top Right: *Oncidium onustum.* Yellows and ochres are more characteristic of Oncidiums than probably any other orchid group. This hybrid has attained a particularly pure colour, but most are patterned. Sprays of small yellow flowers are especially typical of the soft-leaved Oncidiums.

Right: *Oncidium* Josephine. This 1966 cross (*Onc. haematochilum* x *Onc. luridum*) has endured well. The flowers, with their larger size and darker shades, show mule-eared ancestry.

Above: *Oncidium* Lillian Oka. The pendulous semi-terete leaves can been seen in this picture. *Onc.* Lillian Oka is what is called a primary cross, since both the parents are species (*Onc. stacyi* x *Onc. lanceanum*).

Top Left: An equitant Oncidium. These delicate clusters of small flowers, poised clear of the leaves, show why Oncidium flowers are sometimes described as 'dancing ladies'. Equitant Oncidiums usually have bright colour patterns.

Left: *Oncidium kramerianum*. A mule-eared species, the striking flowers 10 cm or more high are amongst the largest of any Oncidium, but carried only one at a time, high over the plant. A very similar species, but with a more descriptive name, is *Onc. papilio*. Its name means butterfly Oncidium.

Oncidium (Terete-leaved)

The leaves of these orchids are more or less cylindrical, long and succulent, with a groove on the upper surface. The flowers are similar to those of soft-leaved Oncidiums.

Regime

The plants need light shade. The leaves tend to hang down, and the plants do well hanging on rafts to allow this.

Oncidium (Equitant)

These are miniature plants, with a few rather fleshy narrow leaves completely covering the stem. The plants form clumps. The flower spikes are long and hold the clusters of small flowers clear of the leaves.

Regime

These plants need light shade.

Top Right: *Cirrhopetalum picturingatum* 'T Orchids'. The semicircle of flowers all open together is very characteristic of Cirrhopetalum, and is what distinguishes this genus from Bulbophyllum. In both cases the plants have small pseudobulbs each with a single leaf. Very few hybrids with Cirrhopetalum or Bulbophyllum have been made; these plants are mostly grown as botanicals. They need shade, and grow best on logs or rafts where they have space to spread. The flowers are not usually large, and are often unpleasantly scented. However, the best are curious and striking.

Centre Right: *Bulbophyllum vaginatum.* This Malaysian species flowers gregariously — many plants in the same area flower simultaneously, with obvious benefits for cross-pollination by insects. Such mass flowering is usually triggered by changes in the weather. This species lives in quite exposed places and will tolerate a lot of sun.

Right: *Bulbophyllum lobbii.* One of the largest and most spectacular of Bulbophyllums, the single flower is up to 10 cm across. It was named in 1847 after Thomas Lobb, a collector in Indonesia.

OTHER EPIPHYTIC GROUPS

Bulbophyllum

Regime

Shade or light shade is needed.

Catasetum
Regime
These plants need light or full shade and are best hung. The leaves of Catasetum are plicate, and are a little susceptible to excessive sun or strong fertilizer. The leaves are often shed after flowering, when the plant should be watered less frequently.

Coelogyne
These plants consist of a series of oval pseudobulbs often spaced out along a rhizome. Each pseudobulb carries one or two leaves only. The plants cling to their support by roots growing on the rhizome.
Regime
These plants flourish in regimes ranging from shade to nearly full sun. The creeping habit of the plants makes management difficult in pots, so hanging baskets or logs are preferable. Water well when growing and less at other times. They may need drying out to promote flowering.

Cymbidium
These are bulky untidy plants, forming large clumps of leathery strap-like leaves which usually cover the pseudobulbs. Flower spikes may be erect or hanging.

Top Left: *Catasetum* Orchidglade 'Orchidglade II'. These are male flowers. The exotic looking waxy flowers possess a trigger mechanism, so that when an insect enters the flower, the pollinia are shot out and stick to it.

Left: Catasetum, female flowers. This is one of the few orchid genera with different male and female flower forms; the female flowers are rather less spectacular than the male.

Regime

The plants benefit from extremely varied regimes, ranging from light shade to high sun. Some wild Cymbidiums are lithophytic and all require good drainage for their stout roots.

Right: *Cymbidium atropurpureum*. The drooping spray of rather small flowers with their narrow tepals is typical of tropical Cymbidiums. Temperate growing Cymbidiums are usually larger and much more spectacular (an example is shown on page 116).

Below: *Coelogyne mayeriana*. The strikingly marked greenish flowers with delicate black detailing make this Coleogyne species much sought after by growers. The most spectacular Coelogyne species come from higher altitudes and need cooler conditions than those which grow in the tropical lowlands. These plants like to be hung on logs, flat pots or baskets, and are difficult to manage in limited space, as they need plenty of room to sprawl.

TERRESTRIAL ORCHIDS
Anoectochilus, Luisia (Haemaria), Goodyera, Macodes (Jewel Orchids)

These foliage plants have leaves patterned with gold veins, and small and inconspicuous flowers.

Regime

These shade terrestrials are grown in moist conditions. Do not allow the potting medium to dry out completely. More than almost any other orchid, these forest floor orchids will not tolerate direct sun, and must be grown in shady conditions.

Paphiopedilum (Lady's Slipper Orchids)

These plants consist of one or a few stems, each stem being quite short with up to about six rather lush leaves. Leaves may be plain green, or mottled grey and dark green. There is no pseudobulb. Usually these orchids are terrestrial or lithophytic, with hairy brown roots that bury themselves in the potting mixture. The flowers have a very characteristic shoe-shaped lip, hence the popular name. Flowering is from the end of the stem. There are one or a few flowers per inflorescence.

Top Left: *Macodes petola*. One of the Jewel Orchids; the name refers to the irridescent metallic colouring on the leaves. The plants are grown for their foliage, rather than for their small flowers.

Centre Left: A Paphiopedilum, or Lady's Slipper Orchid. The shape of the lip gives these plants their popular name. The compact mottled leaves make the plant attractive even when not flowering.

Left: *Paphiopedilum godefroyae* var *leucochilum*. The plant has mottled grey-green leaves, and a short flower stalk. It is one of the easier Paphiopedilums to grow in the tropical lowlands.

Regime

These plants are shade terrestrials and need plenty of moisture. Many need cool conditions and do not thrive in the lowlands. They have a reputation for growing well under artificial light. Imported plants bred in temperate countries are sometimes available, but are hard to manage.

Top: *Paphiopedilum phillipinensis*. The long twisted petals may reach up to 30 cm in a few species of this type; those in this photograph are more modest at about 10 cm each.

Right: *Paphiopedilum hennisianum*. The green-striped upper sepal is appropriately called the flag; the two lower sepals are fused to form a single synsepalum not visible in this photograph but lying behind the lip.

Below: *Paphiopedilum milmanii*. The single synsepalum lying behind the lip is visible here.

Spathoglottis

The pseudobulbs each have a few pleated leaves up to about 50 cm long. The leaf bases cover the pseudobulbs.

The inflorescence is erect and well clear of the plant with several flowers open at a time. It rises from the base of the pseudobulb.

Regime

These full sun terrestrials can be grown in beds or pots.

Left: *Spathoglottis plicata.* Grown in South East Asia for many years, this easy-to-grow terrestrial orchid is still common in the wild. Not all varieties are as fine in shape and colour as this one.

Below: Spathoglottis hybrids were the first ever made with sterile culture techniques in Singapore or Malaysia. Breeders sought to improve the shape and to vary the colouring, sometimes by using yellow species.

OTHER TERRESTRIAL GROUPS
Arundina, Bromheadia
The stems are tall (one to two m) and thin (less than one cm diameter), with thin green grass-like or leathery leaves along the stem. The flowers are short-lived, at the end of the stem, one or two at a time, over a long period.
Regime
These full sun terrestrials can be grown in pots or beds. In beds they become very hardy and can grow very large.

Right: *Bromheadia finlaysonianum.* A close-up of the flowers.

Bottom Right: *Bromheadia finlaysonianum.* The flowers fade on the afternoon of the day they open, and this plant, still common as a wild terrestrial in Singapore and Malaysia, is thus little cultivated. However, for those who inspect their plants as an early morning pleasure, it deserves consideration. The plants will grow in sun or light shade, and flower very frequently.

Below: *Arundina graminifolia.* The flowers have a large lip and superficially look a little like a Cattleya, but the terrestrial plant with its tall stems and grass-like leaves and stems is quite different. Only one or two flowers are produced at a time, but the inflorescence goes on producing flowers for some months. The plants will grow in beds in full sun.

Calanthe, Habenaria, Pecteilis
Regime
These are shade terrestrials.

Cymbidium
Regime
These light shade plants are often grown in more temperate countries for their showy flowers. A few tropical species are cultivated. They have oval pseudobulbs with grass-like leaves.

Top Left: *Calanthe veratrifolium.* A shade-loving terrestrial orchid, this beautiful species is also grown under glass in temperate countries. The lip of the flower with its lobes is thrust forward, while the tepals are turned back. The lobed lip is very typical of Calanthe.

Left: *Pecteilis susannae* (formerly *Habenaria susannae*). This striking terrestrial is one of the best known Pecteilis. This one was photographed at 700 metres, and although it will grow in the lowlands, it prefers cooler nights. Some shade is needed, and less water when the plant is not growing.

Below: *Cymbidium rubrigenum* x *Cymbidium ensifolium.* The terrestrial Cymbidiums have oval pseudobulbs and thin grass-like leaves.

Epidendrum (Reed Form)
The plants are similar to Bromheadia, but the flowers form a cluster at the end of the stem and last for over a week.

Regime
The plants enjoy light shade. Grow in pots in a well drained soil.

Peristeria
Regime
P. elata will grow in the tropical lowlands. Light shade and a well drained potting mixture are required.

Phaius, Eulophia
Regime
These plants grow in light shade.

Top Right: *Peristeria elata*. This plant, native to South America, grows well in the tropical lowlands, but is not often seen in cultivation. It needs light shade and a well drained potting mixture.

Right: *Phaius tankervilleae*. This terrestrial will stand quite a lot of sun, but light shade may be needed for other Phaius plants.

Below: A 'reed Epidendrum', *Epidendrum* Alii. These Epidendrums are grown as terrestrials. The stems are thin with many leaves alternating along their length, and a cluster of flowers at the end. They often show brilliant red or orange coloration. The flowers open with the lip uppermost, and last over a week. Light shade or almost full sun is tolerated. The plants grow well in burnt earth.

Chapter Three

Principles of Cultivation

Orchids are easy to grow if the right conditions are provided. In fact, many are very hardy plants. However, different orchids do have different requirements, so the right cultural conditions have to be found for the particular plants one is growing. The most important factors are the amount of sun or shade; watering, humidity and ventilation; potting and bedding materials; and nutrition.

THE AMOUNT OF SUN

The amount of light an orchid receives critically affects both growth and flowering. Some orchids require exposure to continuous full sunshine to flourish and flower. Others will die if given such treatment. Light is so important, that it is the basis of cultivation regimes.

Light Intensity

When considering light and shade, think in terms of light intensity, not in terms of continuous periods of sun alternating with continuous periods of shade. Controlling light should be a matter of varying the intensity of the shading and not just its timing. Fifty per cent shade does not mean having the plants in full sun for half a day and in full shade the other half, though

sadly this is exactly the condition that often obtains on east- or west-facing balconies. Such an alternation of sun and shade will kill plants that do not tolerate high sun. Therefore, whatever the sunlight hours at a given site, the level of shading during those hours has to be adjusted to be right for the plants. For this reason, the beginner is well advised to consider the sunshine and shade possibilities of his or her home before any purchase is made, as it is the major factor that limits what can be grown.

Except for full sun orchids, the plants will definitely require some shading. Shading should be intermittent or dappled. It can be provided by suspending plastic netting screens over the plants, or by hanging them under a tree or in an orchid shed or pergola with roofing bars. Roofing bars should run north-south so that as the sun moves during the day, the shadows of the bars move across the plants. Roofing bars alone will not usually provide

Opposite: A well grown Ascocenda in full bloom. Getting a really good display of flowers means paying attention to all the different factors that affect the plant.

Left: Roofing bars add to the shade provided by the netting in this pergola. If such bars run roughly north-south, their shadows will travel from west to east across the plants, thus reducing local over-heating. Unless the bars are close together, they will need to be supplemented with netting, as here.

Right: Netting is usually made of durable plastic, and comes in black or green. The mesh density varies. For light shade a single layer is usually sufficient, two layers or even three may be needed for shade-loving plants. Netting tends to droop after a while if it is not stretched and nailed or weighted down. The plants are Kagawaras, which like light shade, though they can often be hardened off to stand full sun.

needed during the afternoon. This means that growers who can only get sunlight for half a day are virtually confined to plants that like light shade or full shade. Plants that need some shade will also need some protection from direct sun. High sun plants will grow but may not flower very freely in these conditions.

sufficient shading except for plants that tolerate a high sun regime. Netting provides the best solution because it is designed to allow penetration of a specified percentage of light, and more than one layer can be used if heavier shade is needed.

Morning and Evening Sun

Morning sun is generally preferable to evening sun. East-facing sites are always best. Even shade epiphytes or terrestrials will tolerate some morning sun, and can be given shade for the rest of the day. The reverse — morning shade and afternoon sun — is less satisfactory but may be unavoidable, in which case light shade would be

Adapting to Light

As a rule, a plant will grow and flower better at the maximum light level it tolerates. Therefore, plants should be given as much light as they will stand. A plant with insufficient light will tend to have rather dark, lush foliage. A light shade of green and harder leaves indicate the right light level. Too much sun leads to yellowish foliage, or whitish scorch marks on the leaves.

A plant used to shade takes time to adapt to a sunnier position. Therefore a plant that seems to need more light should not be moved abruptly into a very sunny spot, but gradually moved in steps over several weeks. This process is known as hardening off.

WATERING, HUMIDITY AND VENTILATION

Watering is second only to light as a force for success or failure in orchid cultivation. Too much water encourages fungal and bacterial infections; too little stunts the plant. The former is more often fatal than the latter, and it is usually better to water too little than too much. However, the real aim is to get the watering just right.

Orchids are often able to tolerate a spell without water. Some of them actually require a dry spell to flower. During a long dry spell such plants become dormant or quiescent, with no sign of growth at the root tips or the crowns. In many cases leaves are shed. However, many tropical orchids will not tolerate drying out for more than a few days. This reflects their origin in climates without marked seasons.

The aim of watering is to create a humid environment, and not just to provide water for the roots to absorb. Very few if any orchids tolerate continuously wet conditions for the roots. They cannot be grown with the pot standing in water in a tray or saucer. Orchid roots are succulent and thick compared with those of other plants. They usually do best with soaking once or twice daily, with very good drainage that allows surplus water to run away, leaving the roots in a humid but well aerated environment. This is why epiphytic orchids are grown in very open potting mixtures such as charcoal or polystyrene lumps, or in baskets with the roots exposed. Even terrestrial plants and climbers require good drainage.

As a rule, therefore, frequent watering with a very open potting medium

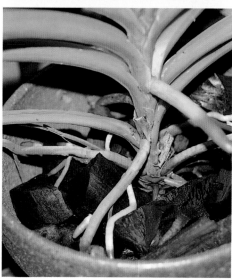

is needed for tropical lowland orchids. This is especially so if the plant is growing on a raft of fern root, a piece of wood or coconut husk, or in an open basket. Frequent watering helps to dampen the growing area generally. This is valuable if the plant is growing in a dry area such as on a balcony or over a concrete floor, or if it is in a very windy place. Orchids generally like a relatively humid environment that is not too drying, and it is less satisfactory to have them in a dry place with only the roots in their pot kept damp.

Most orchids that flourish in the tropical lowlands are those that have relatively continuous growth. However, the best results are obtained if watering is varied to give plants more water when in active growth, and less when growth is suspended. A plant in active growth is one in which new leaves are being produced, and root growth is evident.

The condition of the roots is actually a very good guide as to the state of the plant. An active plant will have new root growth, and the ends of exposed roots will be green or purplish. The presence of such growing tips is a sign that the plant is in active growth and will benefit from watering and fertilizers. A few centimetres from the tip, the new roots will be covered with new silvery-grey skin (velamen). If a plant is resting, however, the velamen will extend almost to the tips of the roots.

Top: Dormant roots. These roots are not growing. The velamen extends to the tips.

Left: Active healthy roots. Note the green tips of the growing roots, and the silvery white velamen surface of newly produced roots.

It is sometimes mistakenly thought that only the root tips absorb water. The roots of orchids can absorb a large amount of water quite rapidly along the whole length of the root. Even old roots, if cut, will often be succulent and green. Such roots still soak up water, as can be seen by the naked eye with careful observation.

When to Water

The morning and early evening are the best times to water. One might think that it would cool the plants to water them in sunlight during the day, but at this time any water in the crown of the plants heats up and can quickly kill the growing leaves.

Watering in the morning is better than in the evening as plants are at greater risk of fungal infections if wet at night. In practice the danger is less if there are evening breezes to dry the plants, and if the grower sprays fungicide occasionally as a preventive measure. From time to time outdoor plants will be rained on at night, and the grower will take into account any natural rainfall in his watering schedule.

Is Tap Water Suitable?

Books on temperate orchid growing often stress the need for natural rainwater, because otherwise dissolved salts may build up in the orchid pots. However, tropical growers use so much water that this consideration is not a problem. If the chlorine levels are high, it is better to use water that has been standing for a time in a tank, and collected natural rainwater will avoid any problem of chlorine or other dissolved chemicals, provided the atmosphere is clean. However, standing water attracts mosquitoes, and as chemical control of these pests cannot be used in the water, fish that eat mosquito larvae have to be kept instead, which can be troublesome.

Ventilation

Stagnant air encourages the growth of fungal infections. A light breeze or air movement is therefore ideal for keeping infection down. Air movement also has a drying effect. In very windy positions such as balconies, protection from drying is needed, and watering may need to be more frequent than in more sheltered spots. Outdoor growers seldom if ever have to resort to fans to keep the air moving, but it is important to know that a very still atmosphere is unhealthy for orchids if it is also damp.

Watering: Some Rules of Thumb

• In a small collection, water plants on an individual basis, not indiscriminately, so that watering is adjusted to the needs of each plant.

• A hot dry environment and a permanently wet one are both unsuitable. A fresh moist atmosphere with good air circulation but without excessive wind is ideal.

• Do not water plants in full sunlight, as water in the leaves may heat up and damage the plant.

• Morning watering is preferable to evening watering.

• Water generously, drenching the plant, or not at all. A dribble of water is not much help. If in doubt, refrain. Most orchids can stand drying out, and prefer it to being too moist all the time.

• Roots can rot if the potting material is too wet. Repot the plants, and ruthlessly prune away all dead roots, if signs of rotting roots are found.

POTTING AND BEDDING MATERIALS

The aim of potting is to provide a confined space for the roots in conditions that favour healthy growth. The interior of the pot is a microclimate, and the aim of the potting material (or 'potting medium') is to provide a reasonably lasting combination of moisture and aeration to form a suitable microclimate.

Epiphytic Orchids

Epiphytic orchid roots require plenty of air and can usually become completely dry without any harm. Epiphytic orchids naturally grow on trees, and their roots both support them and absorb water and dissolved nutrients. However, these roots are often exposed to air, and even where they grow into crevices or under dead bark, they remain well aerated. Orchid roots are relatively thick and succulent, and cling to the surfaces over which they grow. They do not tolerate excessive moisture or prolonged immersion in water, so when epiphytic orchids are grown in pots, the potting material must allow for ample air spaces and free drainage. At the same time a moist atmosphere should be present. Therefore, epiphytic orchids need a potting medium that retains moisture when it is soaked, gradually releasing it to maintain a moist but well aerated environment for the roots. This means porous material that soaks up water and releases it slowly as vapour, while not becoming soggy.

Potting Materials for Epiphytes

Unlike their counterparts in temperate countries, growers in the tropics have a naturally high humidity in the air. Therefore potting mixtures advised in books for temperate growers are not suitable in the tropics, as they usually emphasize materials such as peat or tree bark which retain too much moisture for tropical use. Plants grown on such mediums would be rather soggy unless protected from the rain and watered infrequently. The rate of decay of such materials is also higher in the tropics. The high humidity of the tropical lowlands, and the fact that the orchids can be kept in airy outdoor locations, means that other potting materials are preferable.

Consequently, in tropical climates some apparently rather unpromising but harder wearing materials are used for potting epiphytic orchids. The commonest materials are pieces of charcoal, broken brick, polystyrene lumps or beans, or durable natural materials such as tree fern root. These all have in common a degree of porousness that allows water retention. A combination of charcoal and polystyrene is probably the most common mixture, as polystyrene is cheaper than charcoal and also light, which is an advantage unless the pot needs to be heavy for stability. Most growers agree on the need for at least some charcoal in the mixture as it reduces bacterial action. Broken brick and charcoal, or pure broken brick, is also used, though less than formerly. In fact, as the grower becomes more experienced, he or she will feel inclined to experiment with new potting materials. Such experimentation should obviously be carried out first on plants that are not prized and which have been already grown successfully in more conventional ways.

In using any potting material, there are two essential requirements: the materials should be fresh and clean; and they should be in pieces of the right size. When repotting an orchid, it is best to cut away all dead and decaying roots ruthlessly, and to discard all of the old potting material. Fresh root growth is better achieved in clean materials. Old materials should not be re-used, because algae and bacteria would have built up, and detritus from dead roots and leaves will have washed down into the potting mixture and clogged up the pores.

The size of the materials used depends on the thickness of the roots. The larger their diameter, the larger the pieces of potting material needed for the roots to penetrate, and the more important ventilation of the roots becomes. A large strap-leaved Vanda with roots as thick as pencils will need chunks of charcoal or brick three or four cm across, whereas a plant with thinner roots such as a Cattleya or Dendrobium can receive correspondingly smaller pieces, say two cm. Miniature Dendrobiums and Cattleyas can have even smaller pieces, especially as the pot size will also be small. It is best to have larger pieces at the base of the pot and smaller pieces near the surface. Many growers simply purchase a hammer and a bag of charcoal and proceed to break up an appropriate mix as they need it. For those who hesitate to blacken their hands or who live in flats with a need to avoid indoor dirt, commercially prepared broken brick or charcoal is obtainable. Charcoal should be washed to remove salts and dust. When washed, charcoal is clean to the touch, though it marks if rubbed on a surface.

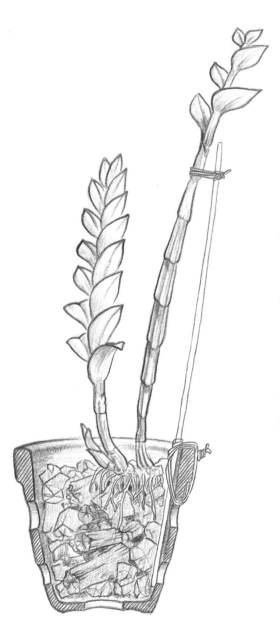

Above: A sympodial orchid secured in position with a potting mixture of charcoal and brick or styrofoam. Note the gradation in size, with larger pieces lower in the pot.

How To Pot Epiphytes

The essentials in potting epiphytes are set out below.

• Have the necessary fresh potting material and container ready, together with any wires, raffia or other material needed. Do not reuse old potting material.

• Remove all old potting material and dead roots.

• Fit any wires for hanging to the new pot before potting.

• The plant must be secure in the pot, and not wobbling or falling over. This means using a wooden stake or a wire support, which may have to be secured to the pot. If the pot is hanging, it is sometimes sufficient to secure the plant to one of the suspending wires. Do not be tempted to make the plant secure by leaving old potting material and a mass of old roots on the plant. Plants grown on rafts or logs or in baskets also need to be tied securely.

• Monopodial orchids are simply placed in the centre of the pot. Sympodial plants, however, should be put at the edge of the pot in such a way that the new shoots are growing (or will grow) towards the

1: Broken brick and charcoal for potting: it helps to have the size you want ready in advance.

3: All the old roots and potting material are removed from the plant.

2: The plant to be repotted should be cut into two divisions. Each should have several pseudobulbs, and should be capable of growing as a separate plant.

4: Soak the divisions for a few minutes in a fungicide solution before repotting. Use gloves, and dispose of the solution on to earth, not into a drain, after use.

centre. The dormant (undeveloped) buds at the base of the most recent pseudobulbs indicate the direction of future growth.

• Pack potting material around the plant, larger pieces at the bottom of the pot.

• A common fault is to see a plant buried too deep in the potting mixture in an effort to keep it secure. When a sympodial orchid is potted, it is essential that the base of the plant be on top of the potting mixture and not buried in it. The roots will grow down into the potting mixture and the new shoots will grow upwards; but the latter must not be buried below the surface of the mixture.

• Another fault is to use excessively large pieces of charcoal or other material. The size of the material can be graded, larger at the bottom of the pot, smaller at the top, and the size should reflect the size of the roots.

• The best time to pot sympodial orchids is when a new shoot has appeared and is just putting out fresh roots.

• To induce new shoots on old pseudobulbs, in order to divide a plant, cut between the pseudobulbs at the points where new shoots are wanted, without removing the plant from its pot. Then, when the new shoots have started, the whole plant is removed, and split into a number of plants, each with a growing shoot. Each plant is then potted separately.

5: Wire the division into a new pot. Stakes can also be used, and the stake may itself need to be wired to the pot for rigidity. Further examples are illustrated in Chapter Four.

6: The potting material is filled in around the base of the plant, but not covering it, and the plant is labelled. Be careful not to discard the old label with the old potting material, unless you have prepared a new one. The new shoots will come from the front of the division (the 'lead'), and will grow towards the centre of the pot; the plant should be positioned accordingly.

Terrestrial Orchids

Unlike epiphytic orchids, terrestrial orchids grow in more conventional soil-based potting mixtures. They grow best when the mixture is well drained with plenty of humus (organic material). They also grow better in relatively deep profile pots. Water poured on to the surface of the soil in a pot should rapidly run out of the bottom. It should not accumulate around the roots. A test for a good soil is that a damp handful squeezed in the fist will not hold its shape when released. Commercial topsoil and burnt earth both pass the hand test, but only for a few months. A good potting medium should pass the test for at least a year. A mixture of about 10% topsoil, 30% well rotted dry compost and 60% coarse sand is suitable for many terrestrials. Paphiopedilums (Lady's Slipper Orchids) may require

3: One of the divisions of the parent plant ready for repotting. Note the choice of a deep pot, higher than wide, for terrestrials.

1: A Spathoglottis plant ready for repotting.

2: The plant is removed from its pot and old potting material discarded. This clump gives two viable divisions.

4: The repotted division.

an even more open mixture with fragments of charcoal or peat added for extra drainage. Some Paphiopedilums are lithophytic, and grow in rock crevices where the roots are relatively exposed.

If terrestrial orchids are to be grown in beds in a garden, similar considerations as regards drainage and medium apply. A bed needs to be well dug and not clogged with clay. Some rubble will provide drainage at the base of the bed.

Climbing Orchids in Beds

Although climbing orchids such as Arachnis, Renanthera and Vanda species and hybrids can be grown in pots, those that require a substantial height to flower usually grow better in beds. They grow strongly and flower well because the relative freedom of a bed allows an extensive root network. The concealed parts of the root systems in such orchids are pale and swollen and form extensive networks, so that well grown plants in large beds grow very strongly. The roots should not be allowed to get soggy.

Bedding material used to consist largely of burnt earth and liberal compost. Dried long grass was favoured by R. E. Holttum. A modern and effective medium is wood chips or shavings from timber yards. Coarser than sawdust, this material retains moisture well yet provides adequate aeration. The bed can consist of a layer of such shavings from 10–20 cm deep, forming a well drained mound of bedding material. Regular weeding is needed, and occasional fungicide spraying to prevent fungus attack.

Beds for climbing orchids can be constructed with brick walls to raise

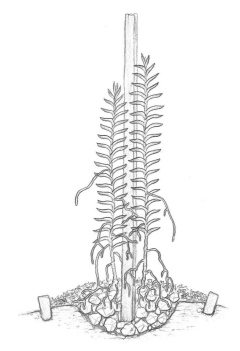

Above: A cross section of a climbing bed.

the bed above ground level. If the bricks are cemented, frequent drainage holes must be left. If such a plant trough is used, a bottom layer of stones or rubble should be used, the upper part being again compost rather than earth. Very satisfactory growth can also be achieved in beds in which the bedding material is simply heaped up on the surface of the ground around the base of the plants. A well drained site is absolutely essential. Drainage is helped by using a raised bed with broken bricks or rubble as the foundation. There must be no standing water in the bottom of the bed.

Climbing plants require stakes or posts as supports, or else they can be supported by horizontal wooden bars stretched between occasional upright supports. Posts should ideally be of a termite-resistant hardwood that will not rot. Creosoted or chemically impregnated wood is not satisfactory as root growth on the surface of the post is inhibited. Horizontal restraining bars are better if the number of plants is sufficient to justify them, as the plants gain support without many posts being needed. Furthermore, the method may induce freer flowering, since plants in this group tend to flower most freely when their tops are above any support.

Pots
In general, unglazed clay pots are preferred for orchid growing. A flatter pot (wide rather than high) is best, and pots with three small holes round the upper edges to permit wires for hanging are useful, as many epiphytic orchids do better when hung. Traditionally clay orchid pots were perforated, with patterns of circular or diamond-shaped holes allowing free access of air, and also allowing the orchid roots to grow on to the outer surface of the pot through the perforations. Such perforated pots are still available, but they are more expensive than plain pots.

These preferences originated in the days before plastic pots were available. In fact, the porous nature of clay pots makes them more suitable in most cases, but where more moisture is required, plastic pots are used very successfully. Some growers make their own perforations in plastic pots using a hot knife. Growers with orchids under cover from rain, or growing in very airy positions such as balconies, sometimes find plastic pots better. There is less demand nowadays for perforated

pots, as a number of commonly grown types such as Dendrobiums seem to be able to grow very well in ordinary pots so long as the potting medium and the watering regime are suitable. Plain pots need a slightly more open potting material to ensure adequate aeration.

Most epiphytic orchids grow better when hanging and such orchids also usually do better in perforated pots. Orchids happy on a bench probably do not really need perforated pots, but the grower must expect the roots to spread well beyond the pot and to cling to the bench. It does little harm to sever these adventitious roots if the orchid is moved, though it may set the plant back slightly. However, orchids are not very tidy plants so far as roots are concerned. As a general rule they do best when allowed to grow undisturbed in a favourable position.

Climbing orchids can be grown in large pots with a coarse brick and charcoal mixture, or with large lumps of burnt earth, provided that a suitable post is provided for support. Several plants can share a container if a greater display of flowers is sought. The roots of climbing orchids, once they enter the potting mixture, like moisture and form an extensive network of pale and swollen root segments. These are healthy. However, standing water is not tolerated. The production of additional aerial adventitious roots that wander in search of a surface for attachment will be quite profuse in a healthy plant, and they cannot usually be restrained into a pot or on to a support. Some control can be gained from the fact that these roots tend to grow away from light.

New pots are best when potting.

Orchid Pots

Pots 1, 2 and 5 are traditional, perforated clay pots allowing maximum ventilation. There is a range of sizes in types 1 and 5. Pots 3 and 4 are plain clay pots, and like the perforated pots have three small holes near the rim for wire hangers. Ordinary garden clay pots lack holes for hangers but can be used for bench orchids. The flatter pots in style 3 are good for Cattleya alliance and Oncidium plants. Pots 6, 7 and 8 are Phalaenopsis pots: the plants grow sideways out of the large hole or holes in the pot. Thumb pots (clay or plastic) are shown in group 10. The basket (9) is made of hardwood and requires hangers with four wires, not the three used for pots.

However, old pots can be reused if they are well scrubbed with a disinfectant and all algae and old roots removed.

NUTRITION:
THE USE OF FERTILIZERS

At one time orchid enthusiasts believed it was not necessary to feed orchids. The philosophy was one of reproducing in cultivation the growth conditions of natural plants, when all nutrients were available through the slow breakdown of natural materials such as bark. However, modern growers are convinced that the moderate use of fertilizers is necessary for the best results. Some fertilizers are organic, that is, their chemical composition includes carbon compounds and they are derived from animal or plant products. Examples are commercial preparations of fish, blood or seaweed. Non-commercial organic fertilizers include diluted urine (about 1 part human urine to 10 or 20 parts water), or water drained from prawn or fish offal, or a suspension of cowdung or pig manure (1 part to 10 or 20). Cowdung water can be applied fresh, but other preparations are better allowed to decompose for up to a week. They are then rather smelly, and although organic fertilizers are often thought to be the best, many growers prefer man-made inorganic fertilizers because they are odourless.

Inorganic fertilizers are sold under

Using Fertilizers

A number of simple rules need to be observed when using fertilizers.

• For most orchids, and certainly for epiphytic orchids, fertilizers should be applied in dilute liquid form. Solid fertilizers will only 'burn' roots or foliage, since they do not disperse within the potting mixture as with ordinary garden plants potted in earth.

• Manufacturers' instructions should be followed for fertilizers sold specifically for orchids. For other fertilizers, it is better to use a weaker solution than would be used for ordinary pot plants.

• Organic fertilizers should only be used in solution to avoid clogging the potting material with damp organic material, which will damage the roots and may start to rot. Cowdung, even in solution, is best used only with climbing or terrestrial orchids, which are more tolerant of wet root conditions.

• Since orchids have to be watered frequently, weak solutions applied several times weekly are more effective than occasional applications of stronger solutions, which simply wash through. Frequent weak fertilization should be the rule.

• Fertilizers should only be applied when the plant is showing signs of root or leaf growth. If a plant is dormant after a period of growth or flowering, it is not advisable to apply fertilizer.

• Fertilizer can be applied as a fine mist on to foliage (foliar feeding) or on to the root system, but it is better to avoid getting fertilizer, especially organic fertilizer, on to the crowns of the plants.

• Fertilizer used for foliar feeding should be even more dilute than usual. Misting is less wasteful of fertilizer than pouring from a container. It is best to spray the lower surfaces of leaves, where absorption is more complete.

• Seedlings require frequent fertilizer, but should have weaker solutions than adult plants.

• Slow release fertilizer pellets of the resin type can be used sparingly with epiphytic or climbing orchids, but fertilizer sticks or other solid fertilizer systems are not advised. Terrestrials potted in earth can be treated much as any other potted plant, however.

many brand names, and contain major proportions of compounds containing three basic elements essential to growth and flowering. These are nitrogen (N), phosphorus (P) and potassium (K). A number of trace elements such as manganese, zinc, iron, boron and molybdenum are also included in the formulae. The ratio of N, P and K is usually prominently displayed on the label, and reflects the balance of these three major elements. Fertilizers high in nitrogen relative to the other elements promote growth. Those with high phosphorus and potassium values promote flowering. Thus a general purpose fertilizer might have an N:P:K: ratio such as 21:21:21, whereas one designed especially to promote flowering will have a higher proportion of P and K. The numbers refer to the percentages of active ingredients.

CULTIVATION REGIMES

The factors of sun and shade, humidity, and potting medium, can be combined to create a number of possible cultural regimes. Each regime is suitable for growing a range of orchids. Although the dedicated grower gives individual attention to plants, it is convenient to group plants in this way according to the most appropriate regime for growing them. Cultivation can still be varied in line with the experience of the individual grower.

The following pages therefore show orchids grouped into cultivation regimes according to their need for sun and shade. Apart from the case of full sun, all sunlight percentages refer to dappled, broken or intermittent exposure to sunlight. When in doubt it is

better to adopt a plan of giving less rather than more sun, and gradually moving the plant to greater sunshine until the best conditions are found. Shade plants are those for which a good measure of shading is always required except possibly the early morning (before 9.00 a.m.).

FULL SUN ORCHIDS
Climbing Orchids in Beds
Generally, these are Arachnis, terete and semi-terete Vandas, Renanthera, Aerides and their hybrids. These include Aeridachnis, Aeridovanda, Aranda, Aranthera, Bokchoonara, Kagawara, Limara, Sappanara, and Yusofara. (See also page 192.)

Regime
These orchids are tall climbing plants which flower only at a metre or more. They require a vertical supporting post or stake, or they can be grown in rows between horizontal bars. They need compost bedding that is well drained, and allows ample space for the root systems. Fresh compost should be added to the beds from time to time.

Water daily in dry weather, but avoid getting water on the crowns in strong sunlight. The compost should be moist but not soggy.

The plants can be cut back when they become too tall for the supports. The top cuttings can be used to replant the bed, provided they have roots.

Full Sun Bench Orchids
These are bed climbers grown as individual pot plants, or monopodials which flower below one metre; also some Dendrobiums of the large 'antelope' (Spatulata) varieties.

Regime

Grow in very well drained large unglazed clay pots. The pot may have perforated walls if desired. Broken brick or charcoal pieces are a good potting medium. The size of the pieces should be in proportion to the size of the roots. Some synthetic materials such as styrofoam chunks may be used. The pots are best on benches to raise the flowers to eye level. Benches also make it easier to control pests such as cockroaches and snails, and to prevent roots rotting. Do not stand the pots in dishes.

Where a small collection of individual climbing orchids is concerned, growing in pots is usually preferred. It allows the plants to be moved, though the roots will wander out of the pots and attach themselves to the bench or other surfaces. Most plants that can be grown in beds can also be grown in pots. Some shorter monopodials and a few sympodials can be grown in this way in full sun. Shorter plants require no support, and will flower before they are tall enough to bend over. Taller plants need a post in the pot. Eventually the top will need to be removed and repotted when the plant becomes too straggly. Such top cuttings must have some aerial roots. The stumps of

monopodials topped in this way usually produce side shoots provided leaves are left on the stumps.

When sympodial orchids are grown in pots in full sun, some hardening of the plants by a gradual increase in sun intensity over a period of weeks may be needed, or the plants may be scorched. Water daily, avoiding the hotter part of the day.

Full Sun Terrestrials

Only the following terrestrial orchids like exposure to full sun: Arundina, Bromheadia, reed Epidendrums, and Spathoglottis.

Regime

These plants can be grown in pots or beds in full sun with well drained loam or burnt earth based potting mixtures. Repotting or renewal of the beds is needed after two or three years.

LIGHT SHADE ORCHIDS
(50%–70% Sun)
Light Shade Bench Orchids

Shading is needed during the middle part of the day. Although some plants may be hardened off to a higher tolerance of sunshine, most thrive better in light shade. Direct sun should be avoided after about 10.00 a.m.

Orchids in this category include Mokara, Oncidium, Renanopsis, Renanstylis, Renantanda (strapleaved), Renanthopsis, Rhynchostylis, Rhynchovanda and Vandaenopsis, also some Dendrobiums and Oncidiums.

Regime

Plants are grown in pots on benches with some light shading during the hottest part of the day. Select potting

Opposite Top: Orchids growing in full sun in a bed. These are a *Vanda* Poepoe 'Diana'. The plants flower best in full sun, and usually when the top of the stem is clear of any supports.

Opposite Bottom: Orchids on benches in full sun. These plants are monopodials and in many cases can also be grown in beds, but as they flower at a lower height, benches raise the flowers to eye level. Full sun sympodials such as the larger cane Dendrobiums are epiphytic and cannot usually be grown in beds.

materials according to the root diameter of the plants, and generally cultivate as for full sun bench orchids. Many epiphytes or climbers that do better with some shade can be hardened gradually to withstand full sun. In the case of monopodial hybrids, shade-loving parents such as strap-leaved Vandas, Phalaenopsis or Ascocentrum tend to reduce sun tolerance in the offspring. These orchids therefore prefer some degree of shade.

Light Shade Hanging Orchids

Many epiphytic orchids do better hanging than on benches. Their sun requirements remain the same. Such orchids include many Ascocenda, Ascocentrum, Cattleya alliance, Dendrobium, Oncidium, Rhynchostylis, Rhynchovanda, and many Phalaenopsis intergenerics.

Regime

These plants are grown in pots, preferably perforated. The plants can also be grown on fern root slabs, coconut husks or similar materials, but watering must be at least twice daily in the latter cases.

Daily watering will normally suffice for potted plants. Watering from mid-morning to mid-afternoon should be avoided, so that the plants are not at risk of damage from water heating up on their leaves.

The potting mixture needs to be more open if pots are not perforated, or if plastic pots are used. Choose pots with holes near the rim for hanging wires.

Light Shade Terrestrials

Orchids such as Bromheadia, Calanthe, Paphiopedilum and Phaius fall into this category, though Bromheadia is quite tolerant of sun, and many Paphiopedilums like more shade.

Regime

Except for Paphiopedilums, these plants grow well in soil-based composts. Burnt earth is commonly used, generally with some loam or peat added. A coarse gravel of charcoal chips can be used to improve drainage. Paphiopedilums need a better drained mixture than the others, and many growers use more charcoal for these orchids. Some also add limestone chips to the mixture, since some Paphiopedilums are lithophytic in limestone areas.

Watering should be done thoroughly when the potting material is nearly dry. Do not allow the plants ever to become completely dry unless they have shed their leaves and are resting. Paphiopedilums do not shed their leaves and should never be allowed to get too dry.

Left: A light shade terrestrial (*Calanthe pulchra*) growing wild.

SHADE-LOVING ORCHIDS
(50% Sun or Less)
Shade Epiphytes
Most Bulbophyllum, Doritis, Dorita-enopsis, Phalaenopsis, and Vanda (strap-leaved) follow this regime.

Regime
These plants should be grown in about 50% shade. Direct sunshine should be avoided after about 9.00 a.m., and heavy netting or other shade protec-tion provided, as the plants are readily scorched by direct sunlight. Plants can be grown in pots or baskets (prefer-ably hanging), or on slabs, and high humidity is needed. Shade epiphytes should be in a sufficiently shaded po-sition so that watering is possible at any time without fear of scorching.

Some strap-leaved Vandas and Doritaenopsis can be hardened off to withstand more sun. The exact amount of shade needed will vary, and all these orchids should be treated with care, as too much sun can be fatal.

Shade Terrestrials
Anoectochilus, Goodyera, Luisia (Haemaria), Macodes, Pecteilis, Paphiopedilum and Peristeria follow this regime.

Regime
These plants should be potted in loam or fibre mixtures which have good drainage. Small pieces of charcoal or styrofoam can be used to assist drain-age. Care requirements are otherwise generally as for light sun terrestrials.

Left: Shade epiphytes. A shady, moist, well-venti-lated spot is needed for shade-loving epiphytes. There is moss growing on the slab just above this *Phalaenopsis gigantea*, which is rather tolerant of damp conditions provided ventilation is good. But beware of fungus attacks in damp areas, or during wetter weather.

Below: Shade terrestrials. Some Paphiopedilums will tolerate only light shade, but most do better with about 50% sunlight or less, such as this group of *Paphiopedilum concolor*.

Chapter Four

Cultivation of Different Orchids

The cultivation regimes described in Chapter Three outline the general style of cultivation for orchids based on their sun tolerance and their type of growth. Basic information about cultivation was given, and particular attention given to potting medium and root aeration. However, more needs to be said about particular groups of orchids, since their individual needs differ greatly. This chapter illustrates and discusses aspects of cultivation from the point of view of the different orchids in cultivation, rather than considering general regimes.

Orchid growers often specialize in particular genera even though the plants may differ in cultural needs. It makes sense, therefore, to give more details of orchid identification and growing under the heads of the different genera. Each of the most popular groups is examined in turn in this chapter. We start with climbers (Vanda-Arachnis tribe), strap-leaved Vandaceous and semi-terete and multigeneric Vandaceous orchids in pots. Then we consider the three large sympodial epiphyte groups, namely the Cattleya alliance, Dendrobiums, and Oncidiums. After this, Paphiopedilums and Phalaenopsis are treated separately as shade-loving groups, and lastly there are some comments on growing species and other particular orchid groups.

Right: Quarter-terete Vandas flowering on tree stumps in the Singapore Botanic Gardens.

Opposite: *Paraphalaenopsis laycockii*. This plant was grown from seed and not collected from the jungle.

73

CLIMBING ORCHIDS: ARACHNIS, VANDA (TERETE), RENANTHERA AND THEIR HYBRIDS

The tall climbing plants in this group are known as the Vanda-Arachnis tribe. They have been hybridized and grown in South East Asia for many years. These are the orchids that more than any others are characteristic of Singapore and Malaysia, particularly the Scorpion Orchids, those with strong Arachnis influence in the shape of the flowers. There are three main groups: the terete Vandas, whose hybrids were the earliest but which are grown less today; the Arandas, which have produced many fine cut-flower varieties such as *Aranda* Christine and which are still being grown and developed; and the Renanthera group of hybrids, such as Renantanda, Renanopsis and Aranthera, which are favoured for their red flowers and spectacular branching sprays. Other genera have been added to these three, giving multigeneric names such as Mokara (Arachnis x Ascocentrum x Vanda), Holttumara (Arachnis x Renanthera x Vanda) and Bokchoonara (Arachnis x Ascocentrum x Phalaenopsis x Vanda). The total number of multigeneric hybrids in the monopodial orchids is over 60. Many multigenerics are not so tall and are less tolerant of full sun than those parent plants that are climbers. We con-

Below: These climbers are planted in wood shavings to form a mulch bed. A similar mulch on a small scale is very suitable for a garden.

sider here those plants that retain the 'classic' climbing orchids' pattern of growth, with tall stems reaching two or more metres if encouraged, that are traditionally grown in sunny beds supported by posts, flowering as they reach the top.

There are many climbing multigenerics. Most plants and flowers show strong influence from one or more of the three major contributing genera in varying degrees.

Arachnis Influence Strong
Examples are Aranda, Mokara, and Laycockara, with
• large flowers with a characteristic 'scorpion' form;
• arching flower sprays;
• flowers in two ranks of the spray;
• strap-shaped leaves;
• yellow, brown and purple colours, with spotting or flecking common.

Vanda Influence Strong
Some Ascocenda, Renantanda and Vandaenopsis are examples of strong Vanda influence. They have
• large flowers with broad tepals but often twisted lateral sepals;
• upright flower sprays;
• flowers which face in all directions on the spray;
• terete or deeply channelled leaves;
• pink, peach and mauve colours.

Top Right: Arachnis influence strong: *Mokara* Willie How. The shape is fuller than for Arachnis itself, but the scorpion shape is still apparent in the flower.

Right: Vanda influence strong: *Vandaenopsis* Prosperitas. The Vanda colour and shape have dominated in this hybrid.

Renanthera Influence Strong

Examples of Renanthera influence are Renantanda, Aranthera, Renanthopsis and Renanopsis, with

• flowers which tend to retain the Renanthera form;
• branching arched or horizontal sprays;
• flowers in two ranks on the spray;
• strap-shaped leaves;
• flowers which are predominantly red or orange.

Cultivation

In appearance, the plants of these climbing orchids are usually either like Arachnis, with strap-shaped leaves, or they may be semi- or quarter-terete as a result of terete Vanda parentage. Cultural requirements are similar in all cases. The roots are quite tolerant of

Above: *Renanthopsis* Dhanabalan (*Renanthopsis* Yee Peng x *Renanthera* Kalsom). Not surprisingly given the parentage, Renanthera influence is strong in both the shape and colour of the flowers.

damp conditions so long as there is drainage. They will rot if there is standing water.

There are several points to note.
• The plants need full sun to flower.
• They can be grown in pots or beds.
• The beds must be well drained. Drainage is improved by a lining of rubble, broken bricks or potshards.
• A raised litter of coarse grass, leaves and similar materials will gradually rot down and provide moisture and shade for roots. Beds of wood shavings or coarse sawdust are effective, but some woods are too acid.

76

• Pot-grown plants can be grown in broken brick and charcoal, or coarse lumps of burnt earth can be used after sieving out dust.
• A post or stake is needed for support to a height of about one metre. The plants will flower more freely once they exceed this.
• Slow release fertilizers can be used in climbing beds, as can organic fertilizers and manures. Pig dung is used by commercial growers. The plants will respond to plenty of feeding once established.
• Water the plants before 9 a.m. or after 4 p.m. Water in the crowns during the day will heat up and destroy them. Daily watering is not essential in established beds.

Vegetative Propagation
Repot or replant when the plants get too tall or lose many lower leaves. Usually the plant is repotted as a top cutting provided that the cutting has roots. Cuttings should be at least 30–50 cm long. The stump will usually produce side shoots provided it is not leafless, and these can also be later detached and bedded out. The plants should be steadied by tying them to posts, or to cross-bars between posts.

Propagation summary
• Repot or plant as top cuttings or side shoots.
• Select cuttings or shoots with two or more developed aerial roots.
• Use a stake or parallel bars to support the plants.
• Give some shade until root growth is established.

Problems
The Vanda-Arachnis tribe are quite hardy, but the flowers are apt to be attacked by beetle larvae and thrips. Plants in beds are apt to be eaten by snails. They can also be attacked rather heavily by scale insects. Old plants may develop root rots. Since growth is rapid, every few years the plants should be cut back and the bed rebuilt from fresh materials. A common cultural fault is rotting of the crowns resulting from water getting on to plants in full sun.

STRAP-LEAVED VANDAS AND RELATED GENERA (VANDOPSIS, ASCOCENTRUM)
This group contains the popular large flowered Vanda hybrids, many of them originating with *Vanda sanderiana* from the Philippines, and their other species parents, many of which are also grown for their attractive flowers.

Vandopsis plants are rather like strap-leaved Vandas, but with fleshier leaves. Ascocentrums are much smaller but have a rather similar habit. They also may have fleshier leaves, especially *Asctm. miniatum.*

Plants in this group need shade. They grow well in humid environments with the roots well exposed. They can be grown in coarse brick and charcoal mixtures in pots on benches, or hanging, in which case they can also be grown in hardwood baskets with little or no potting mixture required. The roots are thick and will grow out of the pot or other container; hanging plants often develop a mass of pendent aerial roots. Such plants do well, but must be kept moist, and this can mean spraying the plants several times daily, since without potting material to retain moisture, the plants

Vanda sanderiana

V. sanderiana is an example of a case where the botanical name, *Euanthe sanderiana,* is not used in the registration of hybrids because of horticultural and historical practice. *E. sanderiana* is one of the most spectacular and beautiful orchid species. It is highly sought after by orchid growers and many thousands of specimens have been collected since it was first discovered. Euanthe is closely related to Vanda, differing only in details of the lip, and *E. sanderiana* is the only species. The early hybrids, such as *V. Ellen Noa* (*E. sanderiana* x *V. dearei*), were given the generic name 'Vandanthe'. However, as the number of hybrids grew rapidly, it became common for them to be simply called Vandas, and although Sander's Lists acknowledge that Euanthe is the correct generic name, for registration and horticultural purposes *E. sanderiana* is treated as if it were *V. sanderiana*.

dry out rather quickly. They will not tolerate wet roots, but do well when hung over wet rather than dry ground.

Cultivation
• The plants are shade- and moisture-loving but like morning sun.
• They like to be hung.
• They like very high humidity.
• If in pots, use large lumps of brick or charcoal.
• If in baskets, more frequent watering will be needed than if pots are used.
• Use plenty of liquid fertilizer.
• Watering is the key to success in growing Vandas. They must be given more or less water according to the microclimate of the roots. The aim is to provide plenty of moisture, but with plenty of good drainage and aeration for the roots. Frequency of watering can be several times daily for plants in baskets or drier spots.

Opposite Top: *Vanda coerulea*. This is as near perfection in blue Vanda shapes as has been achieved.

Opposite Bottom: Strap-leaved Vandas are commonly grown in hanging hardwood baskets. They need plenty of water when grown this way, but the result is a profuse growth of hanging roots, as can also be seen in this picture of plants on a stump.

Repotting Summary for Vandas

• If top cuttings or side shoots are used, ensure that there are at least two, and preferably three, substantial roots attached.
• Dip cut stems into fungicide solution.
• Support the plant by tying it to a stake or to the hanging wires.
• If using a potting medium, fill coarse pieces in around the base of the plant. Any partly buried leaves will soon die and must be removed.
• Keep shaded and not too moist until root growth resumes.

2: The top cutting for potting. The cut base of the plant should be dipped in fungicide.

3: The roots are fitted into the pot, and in this case support the plant with no need for any extra staking.

1: Cutting away the top of the plant for repotting. Ensure enough roots are above the cut. Two roots is usually the safe minimum. The entire base is discarded, as it has no leaves and will not be able to produce a new shoot.

4: Starting to fill up with large chunks of charcoal. These thick roots need a very open potting mixture.

Flowering

One or more flower spikes are produced at a time from leaf axils on the upper part of the stem. Once spikes appear they grow rapidly. If plentiful watering is not maintained, the tip of the growing spike may shrivel prematurely, so that fewer flowers bloom than might have been the case. A spike will grow somewhat towards the light, so the plant is best positioned so that the light leads the spike sideways out of the channel of the leaf. This will display the flowers to best advantage.

Problems

The strap-leaved Vanda species grow quite well in the tropical lowlands, with the exception of some species from higher altitudes, most notably *V. coerulea*. This protected species is much prized for its dominant blue colour, and, like *V. sanderiana*, has been much used in hybridizing. Unfortunately the most spectacular hybrids tend to have one or both of these two species in their ancestry, and grow better when the climate is slightly seasonal, with cooler nights. Such hybrids are not always seen to their best advantage in lowland conditions.

However, an increasing number of hybrids are being reared in lowland conditions, and their tolerance of uniform climate is greater. When buying plants, those that have been raised in the lowlands and flowered there are

Right: *Aeridovanda* T. Iwasaki. On this particular occasion one of the flower sprays has bent around to follow the light, and got tangled in the leaves. The plant should have been placed so that both sprays grew away from the plant towards the light.

Scented Orchids

Many strap-leaved Vandas have an attractive scent that is strongest during the day. For some reason, scent has not been a priority with breeders, who have tried to improve colour, size and shape, but who have given little attention to scent. In the case of strap-leaved Vandas, the use of *V. sanderiana* and *V. coerulea* has dominated the hybrid pedigrees, but these species are not scented, and the result has been large spectacular flowers with little, if any, scent. The popular Ascocendas, which are mostly miniature replicas of the strap-leaved Vandas, likewise lack scent in favour of flat shapely flowers in striking colours. However, many orchids, not just Vandas, have an attractive range of scents — Cattleya, Catasetum, and Aerides in particular. Individual plants in many other genera also have an attractive fragrance, for example *Phalaenopsis violacea*, *Rhynchostylis gigantea*, or *Dendrobium anosmum* (this latter a most strangely named orchid: '*anosmum*' is Latin for 'scentless'!) Some genera, notably Bulbophyllum, have flowers with unpleasant odours. Such flowers are usually pollinated in the wild by flies, attracted by smells more reminiscent of carrion than of sugar. It is probably fair to say that the development of fragrance in orchid hybrids is still awaiting the attention of hybridizers, but for the discriminating amateur, numerous very attractive scented varieties can already be found.

Above: Sooty mould is not serious, but irritating and unsightly. It is not uncommon with strap-leaved Vandas. Gentle wiping with a cotton-wool pad soaked in a detergent suitable for plants will remove it — for example, Physan diluted to the manufacturer's specifications. (For further details see pages 143–4.)

usually a better buy than those that have only recently been brought down from cooler places.

Vegetative propagation is rather slow, because the plants do not grow fast, and aerial roots are not as freely produced as for climbing orchids. Old plants lose their lower leaves but can be slow to produce new roots. This makes them difficult to propagate by top cutting, since the cutting will often require all the leafy part in order to ensure roots are attached. A leafless stump will not produce side shoots, so the plant is not multiplied. Older plants will quite often produce side shoots from the base of the stem, which can be cut away and potted when they have their own roots.

The plants are quite robust and will stand regular spraying with fungicides and insecticides. They are somewhat apt to fall victim of root or crown rots, and are also often infected with a fungus (Guignardia) that leads to unsightly black streaks along the leaves. The roots are rather slow-growing, and if attacked by cockroaches or snails, root growth can be slow to re-establish.

SEMI-TERETE VANDAS AND MULTIGENERIC VANDACEOUS MONOPODIALS GROWN IN POTS

A number of monopodial orchids with Vanda parentage will grow well in pots. Although they often benefit from a supporting post in the pot, and have many similar habits to climbers, they will flower at much lower height than the Vanda-Arachnis tribe of climbing orchids. They can also be grown in beds, but ease of repositioning makes it preferable to grow them in pots. The spread of infection is also cut down when pots are used.

Many orchids in this group have semi-terete or quarter-terete leaves, indicating a parentage including terete Vandas or Paraphalaenopsis.

The table on pages 84–5 gives a listing of multigeneric genera that include Vanda. Renanthera, Aerides and Ascocentrum are also prominent in many of the parentages. Renantheras tend to contribute red or orange colour to the flowers, as do some of the Vanda parent species. The yellow-orange colouring of many South East Asian semi-terete Vanda hybrids comes from the use of *V. Josephine van Brero* (*V. insignis* x *V. teres*) which has a pronounced reddish orange colour. This parent plant is tetraploid, that is, it contains two pairs of chromosomes for each pair normally found in the cells of plants of that genus, or four times the basic chromosome count. Since the chromosomes carry the genes, which are the units of inheritance, a tetraploid plant is usually very dominant as a parent, since it confers an extra set of chromosomes on the offspring.

Below: *Vanda* Dicky Chua. One of the largest and most beautiful quarter-terete Vandas, showing the influence of the tetraploid *V*. Mevr. L. Velthuis parent in its colour and *V. sanderiana* in its shape.

MULTIGENERIC VANDACEOUS NAMES

[Note: Paraphalaenopsis is treated as an equivalent of Phalaenopsis in this list]

Aerascofinetia = Aerides x Ascocentrum x Neofinetia
Alphonsoara = Arachnis x Ascocentrum x Vanda x Vandopsis
Ascovandoritis = Ascocentrum x Doritis x Vanda
Beardara = Ascocentrum x Doritis x Phalaenopsis
Bokchoonara = Arachnis x Ascocentrum x Phalaenopsis x Vanda
Bovonara = Arachnis x Ascocentrum x Rhynchostylis x Vanda
Burkillara = Aerides x Arachnis x Vanda
Carterara = Aerides x Renanthera x Vandopsis
Chewara = Aerides x Renanthera x Rhynchostylis
Christieara = Aerides x Ascocentrum x Vanda
Chuanyenara = Arachnis x Renanthera x Rhynchostylis
Debruyneara = Ascocentrum x Vanda x Luisia
Devereuxara = Ascocentrum x Phalaenopsis x Vanda
Doriellaeopsis = Doritis x Kingiella x Phalaenopsis
Eastonara = Ascocentrum x Gastrochilus x Vanda
Edeara = Arachnis x Phalaenopsis x Renanthera x Vandopsis
Ernestara = Phalaenopsis x Renanthera x Vandopsis
Freedara = Ascoglossum x Renanthera x Vandopsis
Fujioara = Ascocentrum x Trichoglottis x Vanda
Goffara = Luisia x Rhynchostylis x Vanda
Gottererara = Ascocentrum x Renanthera x Vandopsis
Hagerara = Doritis x Phalaenopsis x Vanda
Hanesara = Aerides x Arachnis x Neofinetia
Hausermannara = Doritis x Phalaenopsis x Vandopsis

Hawaiiara = Renanthera x Vanda x Vandopsis
Himoriara = Ascocentrum x Phalaenopsis x Rhynchostylis
Holttumara = Arachnis x Renanthera x Vanda
Hueylihara = Neofinetia x Renanthera x Rhynchostylis
Hugofreedara = Ascocentrum x Doritis x Kingiella
Irvingara = Arachnis x Renanthera x Trichoglottis
Lauara = Ascoglossum x Renanthera x Rhynchostylis
Joannara = Renanthera x Rhynchostylis x Vanda
Kagawaara = Ascocentrum x Renanthera x Vanda
Komkrisara = Ascocentrum x Renanthera x Rhynchostylis
Laycockara = Arachnis x Phalaenopsis x Vandopsis
Leeara = Arachnis x Vanda x Vandopsis
Lewisara = Aerides x Arachnis x Ascocentrum x Vanda
Limara = Arachnis x Renanthera x Vandopsis
Lowsonara = Aerides x Ascocentrum x Rhynchostylis
Lymanara = Aerides x Arachnis x Renanthera
Moirara = Phalaenopsis x Renanthera x Vanda
Mokara = Arachnis x Ascocentrum x Vanda
Nakamotoara = Ascocentrum x Neofinetia x Vanda
Ngara = Arachnis x Ascoglossum x Renanthera
Nobleara = Aerides x Renanthera x Vanda
Nonaara = Aerides x Ascoglossum x Renanthera
Onoara = Ascocentrum x Renanthera x Vanda x Vandopsis
Pageara = Ascocentrum x Luisia x Rhynchostylis
Pantapaara = Ascoglossum x Renanthera x Vanda
Paulsenara = Aerides x Arachnis x Trichoglottis
Pehara = Aerides x Arachnis x Vanda x Vandopsis
Perreiraara = Aerides x Rhynchostylis x Vanda
Ramasamyara = Arachnis x Rhynchostylis x Vanda
Renafinanda = Neofinetia x Renanthera x Vanda
Richardmizutaara = Ascocentrum x Phalaenopsis x Vandopsis
Ridleyara = Arachnis x Trichoglottis x Vanda
Robinara = Aerides x Ascocentrum x Renanthera x Vanda
Rosakirschara = Ascocentrum x Neofinetia x Renanthera
Rumrillara = Ascocentrum x Neofinetia x Rhynchostylis
Sagarikara = Aerides x Arachnis x Rhynchostylis

Bokchoonara Khaw Bian Huat

Sappanara Ahmad Zahab

Mokara Esmaco

Sappanara = Arachnis x Phalaenopsis x Renanthera
Saridestylis = Aerides x Rhynchostylis x Sarcanthus
Shigeuraara = Ascocentrum x Ascoglossum x
    Renanthera x Vanda
Stamariaara = Ascocentrum x Phalaenopsis x
    Renanthera x Vanda
Teohara = Arachnis x Renanthera x Vanda x Vandopsis
Trevorara = Arachnis x Phalaenopsis x Vanda
Vandewegheara = Ascocentrum x Doritis x
    Phalaenopsis x Vanda
Vandofinides = Aerides x Neofinetia x Vanda
Vascostylis = Ascocentrum x Rhynchostylis x Vanda
Wilkinsara = Ascocentrum x Vanda x Vandopsis
Yapara = Phalaenopsis x Rhynchostylis x Vanda
Yoneoara = Renanthera x Rhynchostylis x Vandopsis
Yusofara = Arachnis x Ascocentrum x Renanthera x
    Vanda

Stamariaara Noel.

Various multigenerics. The trend in multigenerics is an ideal of round form, heavy texture, and solid colour. It is becoming harder to guess the parentage just by examining the form of the flower or its typical colours.

Vascostylis Blue Haze.

Lewisara Fatimah Alsagoff 'Zahra' AM/OSSEA

Christieara Rosy Pink

Vanda Tan Chay Yan

This plant was produced in 1952 by Tan Hoon Siang, supposedly by crossing *V. dearei* and *V.* Josephine van Brero. This is the officially registered parentage. The parentage has been questioned, as the hybrid has very flat flowers, that normally neither of the parents have. Opinion remains divided as to whether *V. sanderiana* rather than *V. dearei* was used. *V.* Tan Chay Yan won an RHS Award of Merit and was considered the outstanding regional hybrid of the 1950s. Other similar hybrids followed, often using *V. sanderiana* or its hybrids to add shape and pink tones, for example *V.* Tan Chin Tuan (*V.* Josephine van Brero x *Rothschildiana*). Many hybrids of this type are grown in Singapore and Malaysia.

CATTLEYA ALLIANCE: CATTLEYA, LAELIA, BRASSAVOLA, SOPHRONITIS, EPIDENDRUM, ENCYCLIA AND THEIR HYBRIDS

In the main, the various plants in the Cattleya alliance have similar cultural needs to the Dendrobiums. They occupy equivalent ecological niches in the South American and Asian tropical forests respectively.

Plants in this group usually have only one or a few leaves per pseudobulb. Typically the bulbs are club-shaped, thicker towards the top than the bottom, with leathery leaves at the top. Cattleya plants themselves come in two forms, unifoliate (one leaf per pseudobulb) and bifoliate (two leaves per pseudobulb); other genera in the alliance may have more leaves, and the hybrids therefore have anything in between. Epidendrums, however, (often known as 'reed' Epidendrums) have tall thin stems with many leaves.

Flowers in this group usually have a large and showy lip. The petals are often quite large also, and may have frilled edges. The sepals are less wide, and flowers in the Cattleya alliance are not usually very flat. The flowers are often large, and many plants bear only one or two per pseudobulb. Where there are more flowers per spray, the flowers are typically clustered at the end of the spray rather than spaced out along it. The spray is usually quite short, though some Epidendrums have rather long spikes, and plants of the genus Schomburgkia can develop spikes growing for several metres.

The different genera in the Cattleya alliance contribute various characters to the hybrids. Many hybrids are multigeneric: below are some common examples.

Brassavola x Cattleya = Brassocattleya (Bc). *Brassavola digbyana* has been used in hybridizing for the sake of its spectacular large fringed lip. The

Above: Typical Cattleya alliance plants, on show at the 1992 OSSEA annual show in Singapore.

species *Brassavola nodosa* has also been used, but is mainly grown as a curiosity on account of the unusual form of the flowers.

Laelia x Cattleya = Laeliocattleya (Lc). Cattleya parentage usually contributes larger size, and Laelias contribute colours. However, *Cattleya aurantiaca* has numerous bright orange flowers, and is one of the parents used in developing orange flowered miniature hybrids.

Brassavola x Laelia x Cattleya = Brassolaeliocattleya (Blc). Brassolaeliocattleya plants are among the most widely grown as they combine desirable characteristics of size, colour and form from their various parent plants.

Sophronitis x Cattleya = Sophrocattleya. One Sophronitis, *S. coccinea (= S. grandiflora)* has been used in breeding for its small but brightly coloured vermilion flowers. The plant itself is small, and features in the parentage of many miniatures.

Cultivation
The treatment of Cattleya alliance plants is similar to that for Dendrobiums. The plants grow well if undisturbed, and need not be repotted more than once in several years or even longer if the grower prefers. However, the older pseudobulbs and leaves may become disfigured and unsightly through disease, and many growers repot every few years routinely. Cattleya plants tolerate drought well, and need to have good drainage in the

87

potting medium. They are better grown in shallow perforated pots. Hanging is also advantageous. Cattleyas prefer about 70% sun.

Miniature Cattleya alliance plants are becoming more popular. These will stand a little more sun than the standard plants. They are better grown in rather small pots which seem to encourage flowering.

Vegetative Propagation

Unlike some other sympodial orchids, with the exception of reed Epidendrums most Cattleya alliance plants do not produce offshoot plants from buds high on the pseudobulb. They therefore have to be propagated from complete pseudobulbs with intact, dormant buds visible at the base of the bulbs. When propagating plants by dividing a mature plant, the plant should not be split into single pseudobulbs, but into smaller clumps of three or four bulbs, otherwise the new growth will be weaker.

Pests and Diseases

Cattleya alliance plants seem especially prone to virus diseases, and care should be taken when starting a collection to

---

Top Left: A miniature Cattleya, in which typically the number of flowers is greater than in a full-sized plant, though plant and flowers alike are considerably smaller. This one is *Cattleya* Fireball x *Cattleya* Thospol Spot.

Left: *Encyclia cochleata*. The structure of species orchid flowers is adapted to the requirements of insect pollination in the wild. This sometimes leads to bizarre or unusual forms, as in this example. The whole flower is inverted. 'Cochleata' means 'like an ear', a fanciful reference to the shape of the lip.

select healthy plants. They are affected also by most other pests and diseases, but since cultivation requires that the plants be kept relatively dry between waterings, problems with rots are easily minimized in practice, especially if the plants can be given shelter from the rain. Dry fungal infections such as Anthracnose (see page 143) can be a problem, and prophylactic use of fungicides is needed.

DENDROBIUMS

Dendrobiums are very much beginners' orchids, being mostly hardy and comparatively easy to grow. It is not so easy to make them really flourish and flower, however. The plants are sympodial and come in varied shapes and sizes. As a genus, Dendrobium has about 900 species grouped into about 20 sections. A section is a group of related species. The majority cultivated in the lowland tropics are hybrids between and among the sections Spatulata (formerly Ceratobium) and Phalaenanthe. The Spatulata plants, or antelope Dendrobiums, so called because of their narrow twisted petals which resemble a pair of horns, are mostly native in New Guinea. They are often large plants, with upright pseudobulbs up to a metre and more in height. Some smaller species do exist, and one, *Dendrobium canaliculatum*, is a miniature and is used to create miniature Dendrobium hybrids. Plants with antelope characteristics will often take full or nearly full sun.

Phalaenanthe section plants are fewer, the best known being *Dendrobium phalaenopsis*. The flowers of

Below: *Den.* Jessie Libby x *Den. stratiotes*. The 'antelope' horns characteristic of the *stratiotes* parent are very evident in this picture.

D. phalaenopsis and others in the section have a rounded form that is a complete contrast to the antelope group. The plants themselves are much smaller. Consequently the hybrids between the two sections show a very large range of intermediate shapes and colour combinations and are of a more manageable size than the larger antelopes.

Besides these two major groups, a number of species and hybrids from other groups are sometimes grown, but these are almost all seasonal types, and though they are popular in seasonal climates, and are often extremely beautiful, they are mostly difficult to flower under lowland conditions. They can sometimes be persuaded to flower by drying the plants out or cooling them in the refrigerator over several successive nights.

Cultivation
• Dendrobium plants like high sun or medium shade.
• Smaller plants do well if hung, larger ones are better on benches.
• Unperforated pots are often used and are quite satisfactory for many plants. Pots should be small for the size of the plant.
• A few plants have long pendulous pseudobulbs. Such plants do better on fern root slabs.
• The plants like plenty of fertilizer when growing. Many of them take a rest between successive pseudobulbs. They need less water and no fertilizer when resting.
• Dendrobiums like their roots to be fairly crowded. The pots used are somewhat smaller than one might expect from the size of the plant. This means that if the plants are grown standing rather than hanging, a brick and charcoal mixture is helpful as it gives weight to the pot. The plants need repotting once they become rootbound or if the old roots become soggy or overgrown with algae. Rootbound plants are those in which the pot becomes so full of packed roots that it is difficult for further roots to be accommodated in the pot.
• The base of the plant must be exposed on top of the potting mixture and not buried in it, otherwise the base may rot. This is a common fault with inexperienced efforts to repot top-heavy plants. Although offshoots may be produced from high on buried pseudobulbs, they are much smaller and have to be repotted and separately grown.

The successive pseudobulbs grow rapidly once started, and new root growth is quick. Repotting should be done just as the new root growth is getting started, and it is usually best to remove virtually all the old roots. When the pseudobulb is fully grown, it may flower immediately, or it may flower following a period of rest and drying out. Being generally light-loving plants, flowering is promoted if the plants are given as much sunlight as they will stand without burning. It is not necessary to water Dendrobiums much except when they are in growth, and drying off during the resting phase promotes flowering on older pseudobulbs. The older pseudobulbs should therefore not be cut off, unless they are dead. Dead pseudobulbs are dry, and contain no sap when cut.

Although Dendrobium plants do well in standing pots, they grow best hanging, if they are small enough for this to be possible. Similarly, although some commercial cut-flower varieties can be grown well in solid pots, perforated pots usually give better results, provided watering is generous during the growing period. The plants generally do best where there is a breeze. A successfully grown Dendrobium will usually show a succession of pseudobulbs of equal or increasing size. Decreasing size in an older plant is a sign that the plant is not flourishing and needs to be repotted.

Right: *Den.* Snowfire x *Den.* Polar Queen. The flat round flowers exemplify the influence of *Den. phalaenopsis.*

Below: Mass producing Dendrobiums from old canes. Old pseudobulbs are laid out and the plantlets (*'anaks'* or *'keikis'*) growing from them detached and potted up separately when they have their own roots and two or three bulbs.

Vegetative Propagation

Most Dendrobiums can easily be propagated from old back bulbs. A tip to remember is that if you cut between some of the older pseudobulbs a couple of months before repotting, you may get several new bulbs starting at once from the old plant. Then you can completely separate them when repotting to get several plants, or you can repot them together to get a plant with several new pseudobulbs. Such a plant,

if properly fertilized with high nitrogen fertilizer for growth, should grow strongly and produce another good display when the pseudobulbs mature. At that time you would shift to a fertilizer regime more suitable for flowering. So long as a pseudobulb has an intact bud or 'eye' at the base, it is usually capable of growth. Also, it is often possible to get plantlets budding off from the upper part of the pseudobulb. An old live cane can even be hung up dry with some prospect of sprouting a plant. If such plantlets occur instead of the usual new pseudobulbs, it is a sign of poor cultivation, and may indicate that there is something preventing growth from the base of the pseudobulbs. A common cultural fault is to bury the bases of the pseudobulbs when repotting, to try and steady the plant. This tends to stunt or prevent the growth of new shoots from the base of the old bulbs, and instead, plantlets form from buds near the upper end. Dendrobiums must therefore always be planted with the base of the pseudobulb above the level of the potting medium, and the plant should be kept secure with a stake or a stiff wire.

Above: Plantlets ('*anaks*' or '*keikis*') growing from the upper ends of the pseudobulbs of the parent plant (in pot). The right hand plantlet can be cut off and potted up individually at this stage, as it has more than one pseudobulb of its own, and a new growth is just developing. The one on the left is better left until a further growth appears.

Left: A Dendrobium after it has been repotted. Note that the pseudobulbs are on top of the brick and charcoal potting material, and are not buried in it. The new roots on the front pseudobulb will grow down into the pot and anchor the plant. The wires to hang the pot are fitted to the pot before the plant is put in it, and the plant is tied to these wires higher up (out of the picture) to anchor it firmly in position.

Repotting Summary for Dendrobiums

• Repot when a new pseudobulb has just started to produce roots.
• Cut away all old roots quite drastically, especially all that are not green and fresh when cut.
• Dip plant in fungicide solution.
• Position the plant in the pot so that the new pseudobulb is growing inwards to the centre of the pot.
• Stake or wire the plant to keep it firm in the pot.
• Keep under medium shade and water freely after root growth resumes.

3: The plant ready for repotting.

4: A perforated hanging pot of the right size. The wires have been attached.

1: Removing back bulbs on a Dendrobium. These can be discarded, or hung up in a shady place if they are still alive, so that they may produce a further growth.

5: Tying the plant to the wires to secure it before adding the potting mixture. Note that the plant is positioned at the edge of the pot with the new growth towards the centre.

2: Pruning away all old roots and potting material.

Above: As befits a miniature orchid from a small city state, this cup-sized plant is called is called *Den.* Seletar Microchips. Such miniatures are the new wave in hobby growing for high-rise growers pressed for space.

Miniature Plants

Miniature Dendrobiums are becoming popular, as they require much less space than the traditional forms, and also are delicate and attractive in their own right. *Den. dicuphum, Den. ionoglossum* and *Den. canaliculatum* are among the parent plants used for breeding miniatures. Cultivation of miniatures does not differ much from that of standard plants, but hybrids based on *Den. dicuphum* or *Den. canaliculatum* seem to prefer their roots

to be drier than usual for most hybrids. They grow well on fern root blocks, which lose water fairly rapidly. Such miniatures are also suitable for growing on balconies, which are often drier and breezier than gardens, and where space is at a premium. In such cases they are better grown in pots to prevent too much drying out, and to relieve the owner of the need for frequent watering.

Pests and Diseases
Dendrobiums are subject to attack by mites and weevils, and the flowers are often attacked by thrips, a small insect that damages flower buds. They are also very commonly attacked by *Curvularia* fungus, leading to numerous small black spots on the leaves.

ONCIDIUMS
Like Cattleyas, Oncidiums originally come from South America. They are all sympodial plants, but have little else in common with each other except their characteristic flower shape. Oncidiums come in four groups based on the type of plant; however, hybridization is breaking down these distinctions.

All Oncidiums have highly characteristic flowers, with large lips, the size really being in the central part of the lip (the mid-lobe), which is rounded and prominent. Yellow is the commonest colour and is very typical of this genus. The petals and sepals are rather less prominent, usually being much thinner and sometimes less brightly coloured. Their arrangement around the column and above the lip lends these orchids the name 'dancing ladies', as the overall impression is like a ballroom dancer in a voluminous skirt. The

Above: *Oncidium* Sandy x *Onc.* Taka is a recent yellow Oncidium with unusually pure and intense colour.

Right: An equitant Oncidium.

flowers are mostly small as cultivated orchids go, and very numerous on the sprays, which are long. However, a few species, notably *O. papilio* have large solitary flowers.

Equitant Oncidiums are miniature plants with clumps of shoots entirely leaf-covered and without visible pseudobulbs. The inflorescence rises above the plants, to bear clusters of flowers well clear of the clump of shoots. The flowers are usually small, about one and a half cm across.

Soft-leaved Oncidiums have a flat oval pseudobulb, with thin grass-like leaves at the end, and sometimes also from below the pseudobulb. The sprays of flowers come from the base of the pseudobulb, as in all Oncidiums, and are often very long. The flowers are usually larger than the equitants, two cm or more across. Bright yellow Oncidiums are usually in this group.

With 'mule-eared' Oncidiums, each shoot has several sheaths but only one large leathery leaf. No pseudobulb is visible. The flowers in this group are usually larger.

Terete-leaved Oncidiums produce cylindrical or deeply channelled leaves. The plants are best grown so that the leaves may hang. The leaves can be quite large, approaching one metre in length. Flowers are rather as in the mule-eared group.

Cultivation

Oncidiums in the mule-eared group are the easiest to grow, being tolerant of high levels of sunshine, and also of fertilizers. In fact growers regard the mule-eared plants as quite heavy feeders and they can be given fertilizer every few days. The roots are relatively thick compared with other Oncidiums, requiring a correspondingly open potting mixture. This minimizes the problems of root rot that may otherwise affect them. They will grow on benches or hanging. The flower spikes are long and may need to be supported with a stake.

Oncidiums of the equitant and thin-leaved type need a relatively fine potting medium, as the roots are thin. Pots with a wide but shallow profile are better. There is a danger of roots rotting if the plants are overwatered. Equitant and terete-leaved plants do well on slabs of fern root, which of course maximizes drainage. High-rise growers may find that slabs on balconies are too dry for their plants. These plants do not tolerate so much sun as the mule-eared varieties, and need 50–70% shade. It is always best when fertilizing orchids to use dilute frequent solutions rather than occasional heavy doses, and this is especially true of these

Left: *Onc. ampliatum.* A thin-leaved Oncidium, showing the style of growth, with the flattened fleshy pseudobulbs carrying the larger leaves on the upper part. Many Oncidiums do well with the roots exposed on logs or slabs as in this example.

Below: *Onc.* Green Gold x *Onc. nanum.* This is a mule-eared Oncidium with the leathery leaves, the 'ears', visible here below the flowers.

Oncidiums, which do not tolerate heavy fertilization schedules. Fertilizer should be given at half the manufacturer's recommended concentration for orchids. When in doubt dilute even more.

Terete-leaved Oncidiums also do well on slabs; but they can be grown hanging in pots, if the pot is tipped to allow the leaves to hang down. As with Paraphalaenopsis, if the pot has a very large drainage hole, the plant can be potted so that it hangs down from this hole and the roots grow upwards into the potting mixture.

Vegetative Propagation
Oncidiums usually develop a number of growth leads and form clumps, so dividing and repotting a clump is the usual method of propagation. Tereteleaved and mule-eared types are a little more reluctant to clump, and these types take longer to gain extra plants by division.

Pests and Diseases
Oncidiums are fairly hardy; the problem of root rot is best kept at bay by letting the plants dry out before watering. The grass-leaved and equitant types are quite prone to viral and fungal infections, the latter requiring preventive use of fungicides. As with fertilizers, these are best applied at somewhat lower concentrations than for other orchids, as the thin foliage is apt to suffer if chemicals become concentrated on them.

Small snails that eat the root tips can be a problem, especially for plants grown on slabs. It is a good practice to soak slabs in hot water before use to remove tannin and kill such pests.

Above: Various hanging epiphytes growing under a light shade regime. The yellow flowers in the nearer part of the shelter are Oncidiums. This represents about the minimum shade that the plants will tolerate.

PAPHIOPEDILUMS
Paphiopedilum plants are the Slipper Orchids, *bunga kasut* in Malay, so called from the shoe shape of the lip. The genus used to be called Cypripedium, but this name is now restricted to a group of temperate Slipper Orchids, and the more tropical plants are classed in the genus Paphiopedilum. These are not really plants for beginners. They are difficult to grow in the tropical lowlands, with some exceptions, because most are from more seasonal climates or higher altitudes. However, plants with marmorate (mottled) grey and green leaves and pale rounded flowers on short stalks, tend to be more manageable. Such plants, for example *P. concolor*, are in what is called the Brachypetalum group. Other groups are the Anotopedilum group, in which the plants have long twisted petals; and the Otopedilum group, which is the largest, and in which the lateral petals are rather narrow and there are two

97

Paphiopedilums

The characteristics of this group are
- fused lateral sepals (a synsepalum);
- a shoe-shaped lip with ears in the Otopedilum group;
- often hairy or warty flowers in the Otopedilum and Anotopedilum groups;
- a staminode concealing the pollen;
- a prominent top sepal or 'flag';
- few flowers on a spike;
- the spike rises from the centre of the shoot;
- a sympodial succession of shoots;
- brown hairy roots.

ear-like projections at the base of the 'slipper'. In these latter two groups hybridization has focused on developing the large top petal, or 'flag', which is a distinctive characteristic of the flower.

Cultivation
These orchids are naturally lithophytic or terrestrial, growing in shaded spots in detritus and accumulated leaf mould, though a few are epiphytic (e.g. *P. lowii*). Potting material should therefore contain organic material such as peat moss, fern root fragments, or ordinary potting composts as sold commercially for garden plants. They are best made free-draining through the use of finely broken charcoal. The medium should not be too acid, and some growers use limestone pieces (obtainable from aquarium shops) to help drainage, which must be good, especially for *P. niveum*.
- These plants need shade.
- Repot frequently, say every two years, because the potting medium will deteriorate.

- Do not disturb the roots when repotting, apart from cutting away any dead or rotten material.
- The plants are best with protection from the rain.
- Fertilize only in moderation with dilute liquid fertilizer. Avoid using fertilizers in pellet or powder form as used for garden plants.

Problems
Paphiopedilum plants often fail to thrive, usually because they are not suited to uniformly warm lowland climates, or because the potting mixture is not exactly to their liking. They are also susceptible to a bacterial brown rot *Erwinia cypripedii*. The leaves gradually turn brown, shrivel and die, and eventually the whole plant is killed. The disease can act quite slowly but is very persistent and difficult to cure. The entire plant must be repotted after all infected parts are cut away.

Below: *Paphiopedilum bellatulum*. Good flowers of this species are much sought after. It is not difficult to grow, but commonly suffers from *Cypripedium* brown rot, which is difficult to eradicate once established.

PHALAENOPSIS, DORITIS AND DORITAENOPSIS, KINGIELLA, PARAPHALAENOPSIS

These plants are a distinctive group of monopodial orchids that include some of the most spectacular and showy cultivated orchids. All but Paraphalaenopsis have a characteristic appearance, with a few alternating rather fleshy leaves on a short stem. The leaves tend to droop, and larger varieties are often grown with the stem horizontal and the leaves hanging down. Both plants and flowers come in a range of sizes, from the miniature *Phal. parishii* and *Kingiella decumbens*, with leaves under ten cm long, to *Phal. gigantea*, in which the leaves may approach one metre in mature wild plants. Modern white hybrids may have leaves 40 cm long and flowers 12 cm across, but most hybrids are smaller. Paraphalaenopsis plants, though related to Phalaenopsis, have terete leaves (the so-called 'rat-tailed' Phalaenopsis) up to one metre long. Paraphalaenopsis are officially classed as Phalaenopsis for horticultural purposes, but have distinct differences.

Phalaenopsis plants fall mainly into two groups. The Euphalaenopsis group have large flat flowers on long sprays, often in white or pink. The Stauroglottis group have smaller star-shaped flowers, fewer in number, and often with yellow hues. This simple distinction goes back to 1883. Botanists have subsequently used more elaborate distinctions, but for horticultural purposes the division into two groups is still useful. In addition to the two main groups, the plants of the genus Doritis have small mauve flowers, and this colour is passed on to many of their hybrids with Phalaenopsis, which are known as Doritaenopsis. Kingiella plants are like Doritis.

Above: A collection of Phalaenopsis grown under shade netting, with sprinkler control for watering.

Euphalaenopsis orchids are sometimes called Moth or Moon Orchids, through a fanciful resemblance in the first species to be discovered, *Phal. amabilis*, which has long sprays of rounded white flowers. From this species and others, notably *Phal. equestris* and *Phal. schilleriana* have come a vast number of hybrids with long sprays of flat round flowers in white, pink or bicoloured tones (white with red lips) or with pink candy stripes and spots. These hybrids are now many generations from the parent species, and repeated selection and recombination of the best plants has produced many very spectacular large and showy plants. It is worth noting also that *Phal. schilleriana*, *Phal. lindenii*, *Phal. celebensis* and *Phal. stuartiana* all have silvery marmorations (mottling) on the leaves and make extremely handsome foliage plants when well grown. However, though very attractive in flower as well as in foliage, they all require cool nights to flower. They are thus difficult to flower in tropical lowland conditions without artificial cooling, such as nocturnal air-conditioning. This reluctance to flower is unfortunately often passed on to the many pink hybrids of which they are the parents.

The Phalaenopsis Group

The Phalaenopsis group of plants hybridize quite freely among themselves, except for Paraphalaenopsis. Many novel combinations of stripes, spots or blotches appear when Stauroglottis and Euphalaenopsis plants are crossed. Doritis plants always give pink coloration to their hybrids.

EUPHALAENOPSIS
- Flowers usually grow in two rows facing the same way.
- Flowers may last for more than two months.
- Parent species are white and pink colours.
- Plants like to grow sideways with their leaves hanging down.

STAUROGLOTTIS
- Flowers grow on shorter sprays.
- Flowers are smaller and star-shaped.
- Often only two or three flowers open at a time.
- Flowers face in various directions.
- Flowers usually last less than three weeks.
- Colours and patterns are brown, yellow and mauve.

Top Left: A typical Euphalaenopsis plant (*Phal. Little Mary 'Aloha'*). This one is growing in a plastic pot, which many growers favour.

Left: *Phal.* Toto Han (*Phal.* Golden Buddha x Teoh Tee Teong). A fine example of a Stauroglottis hybrid of good shape and texture, with the striking colour contrast possible for such hybrids.

Opposite: *Paraphalaenopsis laycockii.* This rare orchid is widely regarded as one of the most beautiful of the Paraphalaenopsis group. The flowers are large and have a pleasant pastel coloration. The shape is typical of species in this group, and is unlike any other genus. Paraphalaenopsis plants are used in hybridization programs, as they hybridize well with other Vandaceous orchids. They do not hybridize with Phalaenopsis, which means that the horticultural practice of registering Paraphalaenopsis hybrids as having Phalaenopsis parenentage is anomalous.

DORITIS AND DORITAENOPSIS

- Flowers grow on tall upright sprays sometimes branched.
- Flowers are small with the sepals and petals turned back.
- Several flowers open at a time, as the spike goes on growing.
- Doritis flowers face in all directions round the spray.
- Doritis individual flowers do not last for very long.
- Flowers are pink or mauve.
- Plants like to grow upwards.

PARAPHALAENOPSIS

- Flowers grow on short upright sprays.
- Flowers have twisted or wavy tepals.
- Flowers all open at once.
- Flowers face all round the spray.
- Flowers last quite well.
- Flowers are pink, yellow or brown.
- Plants have terete hanging leaves.

Right: *Doritis pulcherrima.* This species is highly variable. This example has an unusual colour contrast, with splashes of yellow on the tepals. The tepals are characteristically turned back, and this species is used in breeding for the sake of its colour, not its shape or rather small size (2 to 3 cm across the flower).

Cultivation

• The plants are shade-loving and like a good deal of moisture. Doritis and Doritaenopsis will stand a little more sunlight.

• They like good ventilation. This minimizes fungal and bacterial infections. They are therefore best grown hanging, though this is not essential. Doritis and Doritaenopsis are also quite happy on benches. *Doritis pulcherrima* can even be grown in beds as a terrestrial.

• Good pot drainage is essential.

• Phalaenopsis plants are often grown in tilted pots to allow the leaves to hang down, and this also allows water to drain off the crowns, reducing the chances of crown rot. Doritis plants grow better upright.

• Paraphalaenopsis plants can grow upright but are more manageable when grown with the leaves hanging straight down.

• Apart from standard or perforated clay pots with charcoal or brick and charcoal, some growers use plastic pots to increase root humidity.

• Special Phalaenopsis pots with a single large hole in the side through which the plant grows can sometimes be found. They are an effective and elegant alternative to tipping the pots. Such pots have to be hung.

•Phalaenopsis and Paraphalaenopsis plants grow well on hardwood logs or

Top Left: A Phalaenopsis plant growing on a log. Hardwood is needed for reasonable durability. Watering has to be done twice daily.

Left: *Paraphalaenopsis labukensis* growing on a fern root slab mounted on wire mesh. This species is the most recently discovered of the terete-leaved Phalaenopsis.

fern root slabs, but need watering at least twice daily. Successful growth has also been obtained with plants grown on hanging coconut husk or in wooden slat baskets. Coconut husk retains moisture well but rots away rapidly under tropical conditions.

• The plants should not be watered late in the day or they will have damp crowns after dark, which promotes fungi and bacteria. They are best sheltered from rain and dripping water.

• The plants like frequent fertilizer applications, and respond well to organic fertilizers, though these add to the risk of fungal or bacterial infection. Care is needed to avoid getting fertilizer into the crowns, and it should not be applied in wet weather if the plants are exposed to rain.

• Phalaenopsis and Doritis plants grow fast and will stand repotting every two to four years, though this is less necessary if the plant is growing on a raft or log. Species plants are less tolerant of disturbance than hybrids.

• Paraphalaenopsis plants grow very slowly and should be repotted infrequently. The roots can be extensive and untidy, and an effective method of potting is to enlarge the hole in the base of a hanging perforated pot, so that the plant hangs down directly below the pot, with its roots in the pot itself.

Top Right: Phalaenopsis plants on coconut husk rafts, housed on a purpose-built frame. The frame keeps the plants at an angle such that rainwater runs off the plants, but the coconut is well soaked.

Right: A plant of *Phalaenopsis violacea* growing on a tree fern stump. Phalaenopsis plants lend themselves to being grown on slabs or rafts, but sufficient water is essential.

Repotting

When repotting, a substantial part of the root mass can be cut away, including as usual all dead roots and pieces of old potting material. Broken roots resulting from removal from the old pot should be trimmed away. However, the cutback of roots should not be as drastic as for orchids such as Dendrobium or Cattleya where the plants have water storage capacity in the pseudobulbs. Despite their succulent leaves, Phalaenopsis plants tolerate drying out rather poorly, and need sufficient roots to provide for water uptake. Plants suffering from water stress show wrinkling of the leaves, which become floppy. Therefore cut back only to

Below: A Phalaenopsis plant freshly mounted on a fern root slab. The pad of coconut husk provides extra humidity for the roots while the plant establishes itself.

a rootball manageable for the proposed pot. It may be necessary to secure the plant in its new pot if the remaining rootball does not hold it firmly enough. Although the plants can be put in the centre of the pot to grow straight up, they can also be grown at an angle over the side of the pot with the leaves hanging down, and this is particularly suitable if the pot is a perforated one, as new roots from the stem will grow back on to the pot and find their way into it through the perforations. Another alternative is to tilt the pot by hanging it from a single wire.

Phalaenopsis plants do well on hanging slabs, logs or baskets. Slabs or 'rafts' of natural tree fern root are usually used as this material is extremely long-lasting and provides excellent anchorage for orchid roots. However, manufactured substitutes made from compressed wood fibres are available and are a preferable alternative for conservation-minded growers. These substitute slabs are also very acceptable to the orchids. Plants grown in this way need to be secured with raffia or wire until established. As the plants are very apt to dry out until a root system has developed, it is best to provide a pad of material such as coconut husk or fern root over the roots and to keep them moist until they are established. In general, plants grown on fern root slabs or wooden logs require more frequent watering — at least twice daily — than those grown in pots; and plants in perforated clay pots need more water than those in unperforated pots, especially plastic pots. The grower should therefore consider his site and the amount of time he is willing to spend watering when considering how to grow Phalaenopsis.

Repotting Summary for Phalaenopsis

• Repot when new root growth has started.
• Cut away all dead roots and remove all old potting material.
• Leave enough living roots to anchor plant and avoid dehydrating it.
• Dip plant in a fungicide solution.
• Position plant in pot and add potting material, or tie in position on slab or log.
• Keep repotted plant out or rain, and water less frequently until root growth is evident.

4: The plant is tied in position on a cushion of coconut fibre, but this is not essential. The wires for hanging the pot should be attached before the plant is placed in it.

1: This plant has outgrown its pot and active root growth can be seen. This is a good time to repot.

5: Front view of the repotted plant, ready for the potting material to be added.

2: Out of the pot. All old potting material and dead roots should be removed.

3: The plant ready for its new pot after having been dipped in fungicide.

6: Charcoal has been added to the repotted plant. A wedge of coconut fibre prevents the pieces falling out through the hole.

Flowering
Phalaenopsis

Not all Phalaenopsis flower freely in tropical lowland conditions, the main reason being the relatively high night temperatures. Cooling at night is a stimulus to flowering and also increases the size of the flowers. Plants with pink colour (mostly deriving from *Phal. schilleriana*) are tricky to flower in the tropics at low altitudes and artificial cooling may be needed for good results.

Phalaenopsis plants generally produce a single flower spike at a time, but in some hybrids the spikes may flower repeatedly, so that one may end up with multiple spikes in flower on the same plant. This characteristic is found in many species. Sometimes, as in *Phal. gigantea* and *Phal. sumatrana*, an inflorescence periodically produces a further burst of growth and flowering. In other cases, as in *Phal. violacea* and *Phal. cornu-cervi* the inflorescence bears a few flowers at a time in succession over a long period of time before becoming dormant, or often dying. This characteristic tends to be found in their hybrids also. In either case, the grower can choose to refrain from cutting back the inflorescence when the flowers have faded, in the hope of a further flush at the next flowering. With the Euphalaenopsis plants on the other hand,

it is sometimes possible to provoke a fresh spike from the stump of the existing spike by cutting it back to a growth point when the flowers are finished. A flower spike normally has a number of dormant growth points, each covered by a bract, on the part of the inflorescence below that which bears the flowers.

Doritis, Kingiella

Doritis is a genus with two species, *Doritis pulcherrima* and *Doritis antennifera*. It was formerly treated by Holttum as within Phalaenopsis. *Dor. pulcherrima* has been extensively used in hybridization with Phalaenopsis. Doritaenopsis usually have more leaves on the plant than Phalaenopsis, and grow vertically with little tendency for the leaves to droop. The inflorescence tends to be erect and much taller than the plant. The small pink or mauve flowers of *Dor. pulcherrima*, which is the only commonly cultivated species, have been extensively used in hybridizing to import pink coloration into hybrids. The resulting plants are more free-flowering in tropical lowlands than are plants whose pink colour comes from *Phal. schilleriana*, but the flowers tend to be smaller and less rounded in shape. However, they tend to show the branching characteristic of the Doritis parent and are sometimes very free-flowering. The form *Dor. pulcherrima* var *buyssoniana* has much larger flowers and foliage, and has been used in some breeding programs. Doritis plants are not

Left: *Phalaenopsis* Sweet Memory 'Ame Lim' HCC/OSSEA. This hybrid combines the best characteristics of Stauroglottis and Euphalaenopsis plants; it is intermediate in flower size, shape, and presentation.

Above: *Vandaenopsis* Christopher Sng. This beautiful hybrid shows the dominance of the Paraphalenopsis parent (*Paraphalaenopsis serpentilingua*). The other parent is *V*. Harvest Time.

strictly epiphytic in nature, and may also be grown in well drained sandy soil. In general, their cultivation follows that of Phalaenopsis. If hardened off, they will tolerate more sun than Phalaenopsis.

Kingiella is a genus with two species. Botanically it is now called Kingidium, but Kingiella is used for registration.Its interest lies in its miniature size: the leaves are about ten cm long and the flowers very small, only about one cm across. Kingiella is cultivated in the same way as Phalaenopsis.

Paraphalaenopsis
Paraphalaenopsis, though treated by botanists as a separate genus, is kept as Phalaenopsis for hybrid registrations. These orchids are the so-called 'rat-tailed Phalaenopsis' from Borneo. There are

several species, all having long terete leaves that hang down. The plants are somewhat untidy to manage if grown upright, and are better grown hanging from fern root slabs, leaves downwards. They are slow growing plants, requiring about 50% shade and plenty of water. They are still not common in cultivation, but have been used in hybridization with Vanda, and in fact are more interfertile with Vanda than with Phalaenopsis proper, this being one of the grounds on which their separation as a separate genus is suggested. Most Vandaenopsis hybrids and trigeneric hybrids with Phalaenopsis are in fact made with Paraphalaenopsis.

Vegetative Propagation
These orchids are not easy to multiply vegetatively. Because the stems are short, if the top of the plant is cut off with enough roots to survive, it is rare for there to be leaves left for the stump, which consequently dies. Occasionally the lower

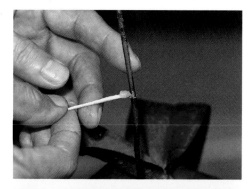

amateur grower, getting several plants to grow from one is not straightforward. Some growers use chemical growth regulators (growth hormones) to induce plantlet formation on the spike or from lateral buds in the leaf axils of the main stem. The method entails preparing a paste of 0.05–0.5% Benzyladenine (= 6-Benzylaminopurine) in lanolin paste, which is then applied to the growth points that it is desired to stimulate, after removal of the covering bracts or sheaths. It takes a couple of weeks before new leaves appear.

Problems

Phalaenopsis plants are especially prone to attack by mites, by weevils, and by rot. The last two are especially danger-ous, in that their attacks are sudden and rapidly fatal if prompt action is not taken. In the case of rots, the affected parts must be cut away and a strong application of fungicide made. Soaking the whole plant in a suitable bactericide and fungicide such as Natriphene is helpful. Where crown rot has occurred, any infected tis-sues must be removed and cut surfaces treated with bactericide or fungicide. In such cases it is uncommon for the crown to survive, but with luck a bud lower down the stem will start to grow as a side shoot. If all leaves are destroyed by infection, however, the plant's chances

part of the stem produces a side shoot, which can be detached and potted separately when sufficiently developed, but this is rare. Similarly, an inflorescence sometimes produces plantlets (also known as *keikis* or *anaks*) instead of flowers, or after flowering. It is also possible to use sections of inflorescence in sterile agar medium to produce such plantlets. However, for the ordinary

Top Left: Applying a paste of Benzyladenine to an exposed node to stimulate production of plantlets from the bud.

Centre Left: Signs of growth; multiple protocorms are visible at the treated node.

Bottom Left: A plant with a well developed plantlet on the inflorescence.

of recovery are slim. This is because the plant has virtually no reserves of food in the stem and cannot survive long without at least one leaf for the photosynthesis of food. Phalaenopsis flowers are also rather susceptible to *Botrytis* fungus attack, which leaves the flowers with grey speckles or patches. This is one reason why the flowers are best protected from the rain.

SPECIES PLANTS AND OTHERS

Most orchids grown today are hybrids, and they are usually easier to grow than species plants. Hybrids are also usually more attractive, considered as flowers, because they have been bred for particular qualities of colour, size or form. For this reason the beginner should start with hybrids. However, many growers also value species plants.

Species plants are valued for many reasons.
• They are often rare.
• They represent a genetic resource for breeding programmes.
• They are natural things not created by humans.

• Many have great beauty in their own right.
• They demonstrate the immense diversity of orchids, and are of botanical interest.
• They are living illustrations of the history of orchid growing and breeding, for they are the ultimate source of the hybrids we see all around us.
• They are a challenge to grow.
• Some are rare or unusual forms or varieties of common species.

Top Right: An unidentified Eria species, photographed in the wild. The genus Eria is related to Dendrobium, with a large number of species in the South East Asian region. However, the flowers are not as showy or long-lasting as the cultivated Dendrobiums, and Erias are not often grown.

Right: *Phalaenopsis gigantea.* Long feared nearly extinct in its natural habitat in Borneo, this species is now being propagated by seed. In cultivation it demands more moisture than almost any other Phalaenopsis, but is fortunately tolerant of prophylactic fungicide spraying. This is a small plant with leaves 30 cm long. Full sized plants may have leaves a metre long and 30 cm wide, hence the scientific name.

The tragedy is that the very qualities of species that have made them sought after have also led to their over-collection. Many orchid species have been exterminated and will never be seen again, and others are in great danger. Much of the danger is due to the destruction of natural habitats, but market demand for species also contributes to their removal from surviving natural habitats.

For this reason, orchid lovers should obtain plants that have been grown from seeds in nurseries rather than gathered from the wild. They should hesitate to purchase plants unless they are likely to be able to care for them. All orchid species are considered as endangered species under the Convention on International Trade in Endangered Species (CITES). This means that in all countries endorsing the Convention, documentation is required for the import or export of any orchid plant. Ideally, all trade in

orchid plants should be confined to seedling plants in sterile flasks. This would encourage propagation of plants through seed and undercut the market for plants gathered from wild habitats.

In growing species, general cultivation regimes do not always apply. Each species has its own limited range of habitats, and growers need to recreate something sufficiently similar to these before the plants will flourish. Some species are much more tolerant than others from this point of view. But in general there is no substitute for knowing about the requirements of the particular species that one is trying to grow, and careful observation of its progress.

Above: *Paphiopedilum javanicum.* The green colour of the flower makes it less conspicuous in its habitat than it seems in the photograph, and it may be that scent or ultra-violet patterns are important in advertising its presence to pollinating insects.

Left: *Eria multiflora.* This Eria is appropriately named 'many flowered ' in Latin. The individual flowers are minute, just a few millimetres across, but the effect of the catkin-like sprays is striking.

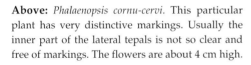

Above: *Phalaenopsis cornu-cervi.* This particular plant has very distinctive markings. Usually the inner part of the lateral tepals is not so clear and free of markings. The flowers are about 4 cm high.

Top Left: *Dimorphorchis lowii.* Formerly *Arachnis lowii,* this unusual orchid has been reclassified. Its new genus name — meaning the orchid with two forms — refers to the fact that the basal flowers on the inflorescence are of a different form and colour from the remainder, as can be seen in the photograph. This characteristic is one this species shares with *Grammatophyllum speciosum.* It also shares the distinction of being one of the world's largest orchids.

Top Right: *Dendrobium lindleyi.* This species prefers a cool dry season to flower well, but this display was prompted by the enforced drying out of the plant for some months.

Right: *Trichoglottis ionosma.* The genus Trichoglottis is related to Vandopsis, and a number of species, of which this is one, have rather attractive flowers.

111

Above: *Aerides lawrenceae*. The largest and most beautiful of the Aerides.

Top Left: *Dendrobium crumenatum*, the Pigeon Orchid. It is a matter of great regret that this beautiful and sweetly scented orchid fades on the very day it opens. Flowering is initiated by a sudden cooling, usually following a rainstorm, and nine days later the flowers open together on all the plants in a given area. This phenomenon of gregarious flowering obviously contributes to more effective insect cross-pollination.

Left: *Rhyncholaelia digbyana*. This species has one of the more curious lips in the orchid world. Native to Mexico and Belize, *Rhyncholaelia digbyana* is known among orchid growers as *Brassavola digbyana*, and is still classed as Brassavola for hybrid registration. It differs from Brassavola in having broad, Cattleya-type leaves.

Aerides, Rhynchostylis

These are monopodial epiphytic species occurring naturally in South East Asia. They hybridize successfully with Arachnis, Vanda and other Vandaceous orchids. Their flowers are small but numerous, and are usually scented, and the long densely packed infloresences have given them the name Foxtail Orchids. They are usually somewhat seasonal in flowering, especially Rhynchostylis, but are not difficult to grow. They have stout roots and can be treated as for strap-leaved Vandas.

Aerides plants tend to branch and like to spread out and hang down. If they can be grown on a tree stump or another large support where they are off the ground and the stems are free to hang, they will grow strongly and give a very plentiful periodic display of flowers. This is especially the case if they are not watered much in the dryer part of the year. The leathery leaves seem to be rather resistant to pests and diseases.

Right: *Rhynchostylis gigantea.* The original Foxtail Orchid. This photograph shows the standard colour form. White and solid red forms are also known.

Below: *Vanda merrillii.* The flowers of this Vanda are sweetly scented, and have a polished waxy texture. It has been used in breeding to give a red colour, but is most attractive in its own right.

Anoectochilus, Goodyera, Luisia (Haemaria), Macodes

These are the Jewel Orchids. They are grown for their beautiful irridescent leaves, as the flowers are rather small and undistinguished. They grow naturally on rocks or in damp shaded places on the jungle floor, and have to be grown in shade. *Luisia (Haemaria) discolor* is the most commonly grown and the easiest to manage. It can be grown indoors as a houseplant, and is always best sheltered from the rain. Potting mixtures can consist of brick and charcoal, or burnt earth, or mixtures of charcoal, peat and burnt earth. As with all terrestrials, plain clay is to be avoided in potting. Other than Luisia, the plants can be tricky to manage and are therefore not recommended for beginners.

Bulbophyllum, Coelogyne

These species have the pseudobulbs on a rhizome, each bulb with one or two leaves (always one in Bulbophyllum). Because the bulbs are often spaced out, the plants need to be grown in baskets or on slabs

Above: *Bulbophyllum nabawanense.* A rare and beautiful species from Sabah.

Left: *Bulbophyllum refractilingue,* also from Sabah.

or logs with plenty of room to grow. This also means regular and frequent watering when in growth. Many are not lowland plants and do not flower freely, but Coelogynes especially are often spectacular and showy if they do. Bulbophyllum plants are less spectacular and usually have small flowers, but are easier to grow and flower. *B. lobii* and *B. patens* are examples of Bulbophyllums with a single large flower; others, in the Cirrhopetalum group, have many small flowers arranged in a characteristic fringe at the end of the inflorescence.

These plants do not take kindly to frequent repotting or disturbance.

Catasetum, Cyanoches

Catasetum plants are native to Central and South America. They are unusual in that they have separate male and female flower forms, whereas virtually all other orchids combine functional male and female organs in the same flower. The pollination mechanism is also unusual: a hair trigger mechanism actually ejects the pollen when it is set off by a visiting insect.

The plants grow best in light shade and need less water when they are not in active growth. The flower spike bends over and may need support. A number of Catasetum hybrids have been made, but many of the species are still favourites in cultivation, notably *Ctsm. pileatum* with striking greenish-white flowers.

Like Catasetum, Cyanoches (Swan Orchids) have separate male and female flower forms. It is the slender neck of the column with its swollen end (the pollinarium) that gives the flowers the appearance of a swan and accounts for the popular name. The cultivation of these plants is similar to that of Catasetum, and follows the general rules for potting epiphytes.

Grammatophyllum, Cymbidium

Grammatophyllum speciosum, which is native to South East Asia, is the largest orchid in the world. Amazingly, it is an epiphyte, growing in trees near rivers or streams. A full grown plant has many pseudobulbs, each up to three metres long and arching over from the base of the plant. Obviously, such plants can only be grown in large gardens, where they require a large raised bed of rubble or rocks to give drainage. They will grow in full or nearly full sun, and flowering is rather sporadic and seasonal. However, the display of flowers, when it occurs, is very spectacular. The flowers are large,

Right: *Catasetum russellianum.* An unusually long inflorescence for this cultivated species plant.

about ten cm across, and a plant in full bloom has many inflorescences each up to two metres long with its many flowers open at once. The flowers are greenish or yellowish with a heavy mottling in reddish-brown, giving the common name of Tiger Orchid.

Other species of Grammatophyllum are not very common in cultivation, though they are of a more normal size. They are related to Cymbidiums, which are also native to the South East Asian area. Cymbidium plants grow into quite bulky masses, which need large pots, or some suitable location on a tree stump. They will tolerate quite high sunlight, but need some shade. Potting material can be bricks and charcoal. Some of the roots will grow upward and out of the pot, forming a stiff, branching mass that traps dead leaves and other things that fall into it. Probably this serves to provide nourishment for the plant in the wild state.

The regional species of Cymbidium are not spectacular, though some, such a *C. atropurpureum*, which has deep maroon-purple flowers, are definitely attractive. The inflorescences are usually hanging, and this means the plants also may have to be hung, or at least grown on high benches so that the flowers clear the ground and can be seen. Temperate

Top Left: *Grammatophyllum speciosum*. The world's most bulky orchid. Amazingly, this plant is epiphytic, growing wild in the crowns of jungle trees. In cultivation, it has to be grown on a rocky bed at ground level. It will grow in full sun or light shade, and flowering tends to be seasonal but not every year.

Left: This temperate Cymbidium will not grow in the tropics, but makes a spectacular cut flower, sometimes available in tropical florists' shops.

Cymbidiums have large showy flowers on erect inflorescences, but the plants do not tolerate the uniform hot and wet climate of the tropical lowlands. *C. ensifolium* is a Chinese species that will grow in tropical conditions. It has upright inflorescences with small, fragrant flowers. It should be grown as a terrestrial in burnt earth with good drainage — some growers use a layer of charcoal in the bottom third of the pot for this purpose.

Spathoglottis

Spathoglottis plants were at one time popular as bedding or pot plants, and a number of hybrids were made. They are showing some signs of a revival of popularity.

Spathoglottis repay careful cultivation, being free-flowering. They are rewarding plants for the beginner to grow. Some varieties are quite small and can readily be grown on balconies. The golden flowered species (*S. aurea, S. affinis*) do not grow or flower so readily in lowland conditions, but *S. plicata*, the common purple Spathoglottis, grows very easily, and has transmitted this robustness to many of its hybrids. Burnt earth is probably the best potting medium, with leaf-mould or compost added. The plants should be allowed to become relatively dry between waterings. They are sensitive to virus infections, which gives a black speckling to the leaves.

Top Right: *Spathoglottis aurea*. This hill species is tricky to grow in the lowlands. It is not uncommon, and can sometimes be seen by the roadside.

Right: A Dendrochilum species growing in the reserve at Mt. Kinabalu, Sabah.

117

Chapter Five

High-Rise Orchid Growing

Growing orchids as balcony plants or as roof plants has always been attempted by inveterate enthusiasts lacking a garden. Many an elderly pot of Cymbidium or straggly Arachnis can still be found, along with scanty bougainvilleas and leathery Kheng Wah plants, in the most unpropitious city sites. However, making orchids flourish under high-rise living conditions requires some care and attention to the pros and cons of the particular site and which plants will grow there. The potential for successful balcony growing is actually quite high, especially given the increasing availability of more or less miniature plants.

Somebody who rents or buys a flat does not usually do so with orchid growing in mind. Rather, he or she is already living in a flat and wants to know how to grow orchids on the balcony or other available space. So the emphasis has to be on adapting principles of growing to the balcony you have, rather than giving a prescription for the ideal balcony that you will never have.

All the basic principles of orchid growing apply on balconies, but certain difficulties arise in the application of those principles. The main difficulties with balconies relate to shortage of space, control over sunlight, and drying breezes.

SPACE LIMITATIONS
Although large plants can be grown, they do take up space, and the high-rise grower is in effect restricted to smaller plants. But there are other considerations too. Planning use of space is important. You will need to consider how your total balcony area is to be divided up between laundry drying and other activities requiring space, or

Opposite and Right: Two successful balconies. The balcony on the right faces east. The plants in this and other photographs in this chapter are shown as they are growing on balconies, and have not been arranged for photographic purposes.

119

furniture such as a table and chairs. If you do not have a balcony but just a window ledge, consider whether plants will impede opening and closing windows and so on.

Having settled on where you intend to put the plants, bearing in mind sun and wind (see below), you will then need to build shelving, benches, or arrangements for hanging pots. If your balcony is narrow, a single shelf about 15 cm below and inside the balcony parapet can be considered. This is about waist height, which is convenient for watering, inspecting the plants and appreciating the blooms. Lowering the shelf 15 cm below the parapet for safety ensures some extra pot support on the outer side. If the balcony does not have a solid parapet but only railings, it may be necessary to block the railings so that pots cannot fall through. At this

height the plants will be visible from inside the flat through the windows. Bear in mind though that the blooms will tend towards the light, and thus will tend to grow outwards over the edge of the balcony, or through the railings, if the sprays are long. Only turn the plants around to enjoy the sprays once the flowers are all opened, otherwise the sprays will bend back to get to the light.

Though tempting, do not construct shelving projecting outside the balcony parapet. Its use would be a hazard to those below and is illegal.

If the width of the balcony permits,

Below: Shelves (staging) just inside the parapet or balcony rails. Several tiers are possible, but they must not exceed the height of the retaining wall or bars. It may be necessary to block the gaps between rails to ensure pots cannot fall through.

Above: Using trellis or mesh on the walls to hang plants. This is a very space-saving method. The walls and floor will get wet, though. Use of wooden or plastic covered mesh will also reduce the chances of rust stains on the wall.

a second shelf can be built below and further out, a step down from the top. This shelf will be more shaded. Alternatively, if suitable, the wall dividing the balcony from the flat can be used to as a site for shelving or to hang pots. Pots can be hung from hooks directly mounted in the wall, or into battens of hardwood mounted for the purpose, in combination with shelving if desired. Another decorative alternative is to mount a robust trellis against the wall, with or without training a creeper on it. Orchid pots can then be hooked on to the trellis.

Even more ambitious growers may find it possible to construct a complete miniature orchid frame with provisions to hang pots or grow them on benches as desired. Ingenuity and a little thought can lead to very effective use of limited space, limited only by one's creativity and the restrictions of relevant regulations.

For those not fortunate enough to have balconies, windowsills will do, but when the plants are watered provision must be made to catch the surplus, so a suitable trough and a means to drain it are needed. Generous watering is always needed with orchids potted in the necessary loose potting materials, since 90% of the water poured on runs straight through. Attempts to grow orchids on windowsills only using spray misting or small trickles of water are likely to result in plants that are too dry.

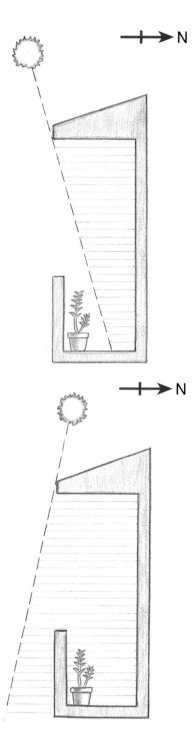

If you are tempted to try growing orchids in the office, note that offices face the problem that many are air-conditioned during the day but not at night. This reverses the cycle of cooler nights that most orchids prefer. It is not known if any orchids like a combination of cooler days, warmer nights, and limited illumination.

SUNLIGHT CONTROL
How much sunlight a balcony gets depends on which way it faces and the architecture of the building. Some balconies are more or less completely shaded. On such balconies it is possible to grow a range of shade orchids. Other balconies are exposed to direct sunlight for at least part of the day, getting more or less according to their orientation and the season of the year. Sunlight shows considerable seasonal variation. North- or South-facing balconies will have seasonal differences in the amount of sunlight.

The seasonal shifts in the sun's path may move the shadow on a balcony a surprising amount, and create great variation in the duration of direct sunlight. It is common to find that a shady spot has become a sunny one through the changes in the sun's path. This can have disastrous effects on the plants if it is not anticipated. It is necessary to provide extra shade or move the plants, possibly by having pots on a trolley rather than a fixed rack or stand. East- or west-facing balconies are spared this variation, but cannot have more than about six hours sunlight per day.

Top: Sunlight in December.

Left: Sunlight in June.

Above: Some plants are in sun while others are in shade. Close attention to the patterns of light and shade, and the changes through the year, are needed to find the best positions for the plants.

Even on quite sunny balconies, full sun genera will not usually flower freely, since the sunlight is almost invariably restricted to some part of the day, either morning or afternoon, or is seasonal. But this means that shading has to be considered anyway. As was discussed in Chapter Three, it is necessary to provide some break or shading from direct sun for those plants that cannot take full sun. To repeat the point, a morning of full sun followed by an afternoon of shade is not the same as 50% sunlight. It is 100% sun followed by 100% shade. So it is necessary to find some means of dappling or breaking the sunlight during those hours when the sun is shining directly on the plants, to avoid burning them.

Shading on balconies can be achieved in various ways. Hardy foliage pot plants can be used as shading plants, or a framework to support vertical or horizontal shading nets can be used. Such shade netting when used vertically can also provide a measure of windbreak. Creepers trained on wires can also be used to provide shade screening and are attractive in their own right. Grilled balconies provide an easy way of adding netting, but such balconies are likely to be shaded anyway unless facing more or less east. Windbreaks are especially helpful if you are growing shade-loving orchids, since they are usually not tolerant of drying conditions, and need good sun protection. However, in all cases, genera that are tolerant of drying out are generally better for balconies.

In any of these arrangements the grower will have to observe regulations governing the use of the balcony.

DRYING BREEZES

High places tend to be windy, and this dehydrates the plants. It can also lead to some damage if plants are hanging and can swing, or if they have long inflorescences that can sway about when a breeze blows. On the other hand, fungal problems created by stagnant air and damp conditions are not usually a problem in high-rise growing.

Coping with Drying Breezes

• Use a less open potting mixture, with unperforated pots for better moisture retention. Plastic pots also keep the mixture moist longer.
• Avoid trying to grow plants on fern root slabs or on logs, or other materials where the roots are mostly exposed.
• Water more often than in less exposed sites.
• Provide some form of windbreak as mentioned above.
• Avoid growing species or hybrids which are especially sensitive to drying out. This includes Jewel Orchids, Paphiopedilums, and many Phalaenopsis.
• Use stakes or wires to provide more rigid support for flower spikes.
• Try growing ferns or other foliage plants beneath the orchids. They thrive on the surplus fertilizer that runs off the orchids on to them, and they help provide a moister environment for the orchids.
• Put down wettable mats.

WATERING

Balconies are usually dry places, since their floors are designed for quick drainage. Concrete, tile or mosaic flooring can get very hot in direct sun, and dries very quickly as it does not retain moisture. The more such a floor can be covered by benching or pots the better. Covering such exposed areas with moisture-retaining material – artificial grass or other kinds of matting for example – should also be considered. Real enthusiasts will find it very helpful to have a tap installed on the balcony. If there is no such convenient supply, water will have to be carried through from elsewhere, which is troublesome. It is also much better, if possible, to allow water to run through pots and drain off on to the floor. Few individuals have the time and patience to take the pots to some place else for watering. Moreover, plants on high-rise sites often need more frequent watering because of drying breezes. For these reasons anything that enhances humidity on the balcony is valuable.

Orchid plants do not like to 'have their feet wet'. Drainage is important, and the pots should never be grown standing in saucers or pans of water to promote humidity. It is permissible to stand pots on trays of gravel, so long as the pots are not actually wet.

ADVANTAGES OF HIGH-RISE GROWING

There are a number of advantages in using balconies. Pests are less of a problem: a collection of orchids on a balcony is more isolated from other plants, and therefore pests are less likely to visit the collection. As well as fewer common pests, such as scale insects, this also means fewer bird droppings, or bees pollinating the flowers. Although domestic pests like ants and cockroaches may still be present, they are much easier to control.

As well as reduced pests, diseases are also less of a problem for balcony

growers. In particular, the disadvantages of breezes are also their advantages in helping to keep the plants free of disease. Restricted space always makes high-rise growers careful about adding to their collections, and it pays off handsomely if such growers only choose healthy pest-free plants. Similarly, weeds are less of a problem, as the seeds do not get to the orchid pots so easily.

A word should be put in here to stress the potential of miniature plants for the balcony or indoor grower. Technically a miniature is a plant which is mature at not more than 15 cm high, but in this book the term is used loosely to refer to any orchid which is small by the standards normally found among orchids of that general type. Growers in temperate climates, faced with expensive heating bills, have often specialized in miniature plants to save space, especially plants that will grow under more temperate conditions. An emphasis on miniatures has not hitherto been a feature of tropical growing,

Above: Mini Cattleyas growing on a shelf built for the purpose just inside the balcony parapet wall.

but there is no reason why it should not be, as the number of would-be growers with restricted space increases. Anyone whose space is limited, even in a garden, can find great satisfaction in miniatures or smaller varieties. These have a great charm of their own and should not at all be thought of as second rate substitutes for larger plants. They are well worth growing in their own right.

It is to be hoped that more individuals will be tempted to attempt growing orchids under high-rise conditions, and will inform OSSEA of their experience, so that the benefits of their efforts can be passed on. It is also our hope that trends to miniaturization, especially in Dendrobiums, Vandas and Oncidiums, will provide the grower with an increasing range of viable windowsill and balcony plants.

Chapter Six

Choosing and Buying Orchids

Orchid buying for the beginner is often a matter of an impulse purchase. A plant in full bloom looks irresistibly attractive and the purchaser is hooked. Or, something small and cheaply priced attracts the eye and tempts one with the possibility of a bargain. Such impulse purchases are part of the fun, but may lead to disappointment if the buyer cannot repeat the spectacular display, or get the plant to flourish under the conditions he can provide. With more experience, the buyer becomes more selective, but even so, there is often a temptation to purchase a plant on the spur of the moment. However, gaining experience can be expensive and frustrating if it is done the hard way. In view of the importance of purchasing plants that are healthy and that will grow in the conditions that can be provided (especially for high-rise growers), this brief chapter suggests some precautions that can be taken.

SEEDLINGS AND YOUNG PLANTS

One can buy orchids from sizes ranging from tiny seedlings to adult flowering plants. It is even possible to buy seedlings in sterile flasks, while they are still too small for even the smallest pot. Young, healthy plants should be robust in their growth. The earlier leaves should still be intact. The new leaves should be progressively larger in size than the older ones. The healthy colour is grass green not dull dark green. The leaf surface both above and below should be unblemished and disease-free.

Orchids can be propagated by a technique called mericloning. All the plants in a mericlone are genetically identical (except for a tiny proportion where a genetic mutation occurs). Since a mericloned plant is grown in culture from a selected parent plant, all such mericlones will be identical to the parent plant. Mericloning is really just a method of mass-producing quality plantlets by vegetative means.

The flowers of plants other than mericlones may show the characteristics of one or other parent or they may be

---

Opposite: An unregistered hybrid. This Yusofara awaits a name, which will be given when the parentage is registered with the Royal Horticultural Society of London. Registrants name their hybrids after friends, relations or VIPs, or give descriptive or whimsical names.

127

intermediate. In some cases novel characteristics may appear. In any case, there will be some uncertainty as to just what the flower will look like. If the cross is a repeat cross, that is, one that has previously been made with the same parentage, the likely outcome in the offspring is known. However, no-one can predict exactly the resulting look for a particular plant, as the offspring of a cross can be quite variable. Much depends on the quality of the actual parent plants used by the breeder.

ADULT PLANTS:
WHAT TO LOOK FOR

When buying fully grown plants the buyer should note a number of points. Look for evidence of recent or current growth, uniform leaf coloration, and green, growing root tips. Many growers

Above: Individual Phalaenopsis seedlings growing on charcoal fragments in plastic pots.

believe the condition of the roots is a better guide than anything else to the condition of the plant, as growing roots are never found on unhealthy or half-dead plants. Look for a free-flowering plant as shown by current flower display, but also by the presence of the stumps of previous flower stalks.

Plants should be well established, with a good root system clinging to the pot. The pot should be clean and the potting material not overgrown with algae, grass or weeds, or clogged with detritus. Whether it be bricks, charcoal, fern root, bark or similar material, the potting material should have a fresh appearance. If it looks 'old' or covered by moulds or green/brown algae then the plants need repotting with new materials, otherwise the roots will suffer and future growth will be stunted.

Pot size in relation to the plant needs consideration especially in the case of

Left: Individual plantlets. Look for healthy plants growing well, like these Aranda mericlone 'seedlings'. All plants this size tend to be described as seedlings, but in this case they have not been grown from seed, but are clones.

Compots

Community pots contain a number of seedlings growing together.

PROS
- There is variety in the offspring.
- There is a greater possibility of getting an outstanding plant.
- A number of plants can be bought cheaply.
- There is no need to deflask seedings.
- Plants in compots have a higher survival rate than seedlings in flasks.
- Weak or stunted plants can be discarded.

CONS
- You will need to pot the seedlings individually as they grow.
- Infections spread more rapidly once started.
- When adult the plants will take up space.
- The plants are more delicate than older seedlings.

Above: Dendrobium seedlings in compots (community pots), each with a dozen or more seedlings. Compots give more plants than individual pots, but a longer wait before they flower. Orchids are slow-growing, and it can take several years before plants in a compot are large enough to flower. Note the lack of a label. Many growers write on the pots themselves with a permanent marker.

sympodial plants. There must be allowance for future growths. On the other hand an oversized container has its disadvantages: growing materials are wasted, more physical space is taken up, and a small plant in too large a pot will take a long time to become firmly established with no movement. Flowering seems to be promoted in smaller pots.

Be wary of recently potted plants. Sometimes one finds a plant that has been repotted for sale, but which has not yet grown new roots into the potting mixture. It is only loosely held in the pot. Such a plant shows the vigour it had in its previous pot, but whether it can be sustained in the new one will depend on the skill of the grower. In particular, top cuttings of Arandas and other climbers are sometimes sold in this way. You may be fascinated by the beautiful blooms of such a plant, but it could be a towering giant flowering for the very first time, with the top portion of 40–90 cm lopped

off and potted up for sale. An easy test to establish if a plant is recently potted is to lift it gently by its stem or pseudobulbs. A recently potted plant will start to come free of the potting material.

Avoid any evidence of neglect or disease, such as leaves discoloured or showing insect damage or bruising, or distorted, or with symptoms of disease (see Chapter Seven). Plants with any kind of virus or disease should be avoided even when they are attractive or seem to be bargains, as they are more trouble than they are worth and may affect other plants. It is far better never to introduce a disease into a garden or balcony than to be faced with the irritating and time-consuming business of eradicating it once established, and perhaps seeing the progress of the plant collection set back by years.

If the plant has flowers on display, selection is easier. Personal preferences in colour, form and size can guide the buyer. Taste in flowers is subjective, so grow what you like. What is fashionable tends to be flowers that are large for the type, relatively flat and round, with good colour combinations and full solid colour; heavy substance and texture (to the touch); good spacing on a pleasingly held inflorescence; and numerous and frequent flowers. However, miniature plants are not expected to have very large flowers, and a certain aesthetic proportion between plant and flowers is desirable, rather than size for the sake of it.

Avoid plants with distorted flowers of poor shape or with bud drop (some yellow, wrinkled or missing buds or some flowers missing from the inflorescence). To know what one is buying, buy only when the plant is in flower. Unflowered seedlings or young plants are more fun because of the element of chance, but beware of being palmed off with hybrids known to be of poor qual-

ity. Note also that large plants with no evidence of having flowered may be shy of flowering and hence unrewarding for the beginner. Frequency of flowering is evidenced by remains of previous flower spikes on the pseudobulbs or in the leaf axils.

It is a good idea to buy only labelled plants. Orchids enjoy an unequalled historical record of hybrids made, and the genealogy of most named hybrids can be ascertained. All serious growers are particular about this. Sometimes just a hybrid name is given; sometimes a hybrid has not yet been named, in which case the parentage should be given (e.g. *Doritaenopsis* Hawakita Beauty x *Phalaenopsis* Mount Ka'ala 'Elegance' AM). In this example, an awarded plant has been used as the pollen parent, as indicated by the letters AM. The plant has previously been awarded an Award of Merit. Such a hybrid carries a certain

What to Look for in Monopodial Orchids

- Note the shape, size, colour and scent of the flowers.
- Check that there is a good arrangement and spacing of flowers on the spike.
- The spike should be long and elegant.
- The buds at the tip of the spike should not be shrivelled.
- Old flower spike stumps are evidence of free flowering.
- Roots should be adequate and healthy, with growing tips.
- Make sure there is a name tag.
- The crown should be healthy.
- The leaves should be turgid and of good colour, with no spots or discoloration.
- The potting material and pot should be clean.
- The plant should be established in the pot.

Sympodials

• Mostly the same points apply as for monopodials.
• Look for new shoots starting at the base of the pseudobulbs.

expectation of quality as a result of its parentage, and may command a correspondingly higher price. However, many hybrids are not from awarded plants, and one learns to rely on the judgement of the breeder and the general standard of his crosses in purchasing.

Some purchasers, and especially first-time buyers, are attracted by a densely flowering commercially supplied plant that shows all the skills and expertise of a professional grower. Often they then find that when the display subsides it is not so easy to repeat the performance. This is especially true for Dendrobiums. Remember that a plant brought to peak condition and then flowering on several

pseudobulbs may need to go through another growth cycle before further flower spikes can be expected. In such cases pay close attention to the condition of the potting material. It may be that the plant will require repotting as soon as flowering is completed, with perhaps removal of one or two back bulbs. You may feel reluctant to repot a fine Dendrobium but if you just keep it undisturbed in the hopes of further flower sprays you may find the performance never repeats the spectacular beauty that lured you into the original purchase. More drastic measures are usually required.

WHERE TO BUY ORCHIDS
The local orchid society is the best place for friendly advice on local suppliers. Many growers advertise in telephone directories or specialist magazines. Going to an orchid show is always a good way of getting in touch with growers and often there will be plants for sale at the show.

Always consider the physical limitations of the growing area. It is easy to underestimate the space required to raise seedlings and small plants to maturity. Consider the sun and shade arrangements that will be needed. The day you stop adding plants to your collection is a sign of waning interest, but the experienced grower is selective in purchasing and is guided by interests in particular genera or types of flower. Few can be indiscriminate growers. But do not allow prosaic considerations to deter you from starting to grow altogether. By the time you have an idea of exactly what further plants you need to refine your collection, this chapter will have become superfluous.

131

Above: A newly registered hybrid, *Phalaenopsis* Asean. This is a cross between *Phal.* Boediardjo x *Phal. denevei*. This is really a Paraphalaenopsis cross, but Paraphalaenopsis is not recognized as different from Phalaenopsis for registration purposes.

Left: One of a huge number of Phalaenopsis hybrids now available to tropical orchid growers.

Opposite Top Right: This wild species (*Phalaenopsis mannii*) is far less showy than most hybrids, but has a certain charm behind a curtain of casuarina leaves.

Opposite Bottom Left: Another beautiful species orchid, *Paraphalaenopsis serpentilingua*, which literally means 'snake's tongue'. These showy orchids are endemic to Borneo, being found nowhere else in the world.

Opposite Bottom Right: An unnamed hybrid, *Phal.* James Leung x *Phal.* David Lim.

Plant Types

There are five kinds of plants.

SPECIES PLANTS

Species orchids are wild plants. They are less spectacular than the hybrids, and harder to grow. Beginners should avoid species orchids collected from the jungle. Many species are threatened by the destruction of habitats, or by overcollecting. Increasingly they are being raised in nurseries from seeds. These are the plants to buy.

NEW HYBRIDS

No one knows just what the flowers will be like in a new hybrid. One or other parent may dominate, or the offspring may show new and unexpected characteristics. New hybrids are continually being produced.

HYBRIDS

The great majority of orchids for sale are plants that have previously flowered, and are known. They should have a name, or a parentage if no name has yet been registered.

REPEAT CROSSES

These are hybrids which repeat a previous cross in an attempt to improve the plants by using better varieties as parents. The results will be more or less known from the earlier cross.

MERICLONED PLANTS

These are quality plants that have been selected and cloned. All the plants are identical, and so the quality of the flowers is ensured. They are not usually very expensive because they are produced in large numbers.

Chapter Seven

Pests and Diseases

Growing healthy orchids requires not only attention to their cultural needs, but also the prevention of attack from disease or damage by insects and other pests. Although mostly quite hardy plants, not quickly or easily killed, orchids often show signs of disease or of insect attacks, especially in the wild. Cultivated orchids are, if anything, even more susceptible to attacks, and proper preventive steps are essential. However, prolonged ill treatment or infection can eventually prove fatal, and some diseases, such as rots, can kill fast once they strike. Symptoms of poor health include premature shedding or discolouring of leaves; rotting of leaves, stems or roots; distorted stems or leaves; poor flowering and general failure to thrive. The causes are various: poor cultivation technique, a poor strain with genetic defects, attack by disease, or pests of various kinds. This chapter provides a general guide to dealing with failures to thrive. It covers viruses, bacterial and fungal infections, pests, and symptoms of poor culture.

VIRUSES

Viruses are infectious disease organisms even more minute than bacteria. They spread from plant to plant by infected sap, for example when a cutting tool is used for a number of plants in succession. Contrary to popular belief, the common viruses are apparently not widely transmitted by aphids or other insects. Insect carriers of viruses are apparently highly specific.

Virus infections are quite common. They do not usually kill the plants, though they weaken them. They involve a greater or lesser degree of leaf discoloration, often with yellow or

Opposite: A mealy bug on a fern leaf. Individually attractive, but an infestation is troublesome.

Right: A snail — beautiful to see, but a threat to your plants.

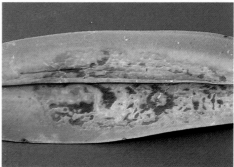

Above: Chlorotic discoloration. Irregular yellow pits, or sometimes a larger area of yellowish patches.

Above: Large yellow and black areas in the centre of the leaf. This is a more severe attack of ringspot virus.

Top: Ringed discoloration: Ondontoglossum Ringspot Virus. It can occur in many different species. This is an Oncidium leaf. The rings of discoloration on the leaves may be yellow, brown or black. (Not to be confused with the banding effect seen in Anthracnose fungal infection, see p. 143).

black mottling or pitting, or ring-shaped or streaked patterns. Sometimes extensive black discoloration and dead (necrotic) patches occur. Viruses can also cause colour and shape abnormalities in the flower. Once infected, there is no cure, and consequently viruses tend to build up in old collections. They can only be eradicated by destroying infected plants and disinfecting the site.

A number of different viruses have been found in cultivated orchids worldwide, but three in particular are a common cause of cultivation problems. These are Cymbidium Mosaic Virus (CyMV), Tobacco Mosaic Virus (Orchid type, TMV-O), and Odontoglossum Ringspot Virus (ORSV). They take their names from the mosaic or ring shaped discolorations they usually produce in leaves. However, they are difficult to diagnose because the same virus may cause different symptoms in different orchid genera. The severity of the symptoms may depend on the condition of the plant. A well cultivated plant may show almost no symptoms, though it remains a source of infection.

Once infected, the whole of a plant

becomes infected. It is weakened but does not die, and may be relatively symptom-free. It is not always easy to know if a virus is present or not, and it may be necessary to have a laboratory test performed. If virus is found there is no cure, so prevention is essential.

The various symptoms of virus infection are shown in the plates.

Top Right: Black speckling. This pattern is seen in Cymbidium and Spathoglottis plants among others. Some fungus infections can give a similar pattern in some orchids, notably Dendrobiums.

Centre Right: Colour break. Irregular streaking or blotching in the flower colour. This is a Cattleya. Note that colour break can also occur in mutant plants as a genetic defect. It should not be confused with the discoloration sometimes seen as a result of damage from thrips, which is a small insect (see p. 150).

Bottom Right: Twisted growth. The elongated distorted growth of the new crown, especially in Dendrobium plants, may be the result of virus infection, or excess fertilizer.

Below: Irregular black mottling. The discoloration on the leaves, which is dead tissue, may be in large blotches and streaks, or smaller spots. Note that other diseases, especially fungus diseases, may also cause various types of black speckling or spotting of leaves. This plant is an Oncidium.

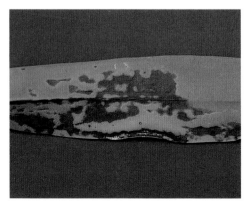

137

Above: Bud drop. The developing buds wilt and drop off. Bud drop may also occur for other reasons, notably water stress when the plant is too dry, or a polluted atmosphere, or if the atmosphere is too damp.

Even though an infected plant may show little sign of infection, it will not recover. The virus remains present, and the plant will be a source of infection for other plants. It is therefore desirable to prevent virus infection from ever getting established in a collection. It is best to be quite ruthless about destroying infected plants. If it is intended to keep valuable or rare infected plants it is best to isolate them, if possible at another site. Otherwise they should at least be kept in a separate part of the collection, and it is better to work with them only after visiting your healthy plants. The fact that virus disease is not curable is one reason why breeding programmes to renew stocks of species plants in cultivation are highly desirable.

The sterilization of cutting tools between each plant is recommended as a way to avoid passing infection from plant to plant. This recommendation is often neglected as it can be troublesome with large collections. Moreover, it is only in recent years that virus infections have been recognized as a widespread problem for orchid growers. However, with many elderly collections in existence, the incidence of viral infection is probably quite high, and rising.

The private grower with a small collection should use sterilization procedures before pruning or cutting any part of the plant, including flower sprays. The best method is to use disposable blades, one per plant. This is not wasteful if the blades are kept and sterilized for reuse, but it is not very practical. The simplest method of quick sterilization is to use a pocket cigarette lighter and flame the edge of any blade before moving on to the next plant. Care must be taken to ensure thorough flaming for several seconds. Use of a small blowlamp for flaming is trickier but very effective. Alternatively, a small pail of horticultural sterilizing solution can be used to douse cutters between plants. The cutter has to be left in the solution for some time, and a better system is to use several cutters with the grower using each in turn as the others soak. Suitable solutions include 20% chlorox solution, 2% sodium hydroxide solution, saturated sodium triphosphate, or a disinfectant such as Physan sold especially for use with plants.

At first it seems troublesome to sterilize blades, but if it is done routinely, it becomes more or less automatic. Flaming with a cigarette lighter is probably the simplest and most effective way of routinely keeping a small collection free from virus.

Questions and Answers on Viruses

WHAT IS A VIRUS?
A virus is too small to be seen even with a microscope. It is an infectious particle made of one or more pieces of ribonucleic acid (RNA) or deoxyribonucleic acid (DNA), surrounded by proteins. Viruses cannot multiply on their own and can only exist as parasites.

IS THERE MORE THAN ONE KIND OF ORCHID VIRUS?
For cultivated orchids some 18 viruses have been reported. Cymbidium Mosaic Virus (CyMV), Tobacco Mosaic Virus (TMV-O) and Odontoglossum Ringspot Virus (ORSV) are found worldwide. Rhabdo (bullet-shaped) viruses have also been reported.

CAN A VIRUS-INFECTED PLANT BE CURED?
No, once a plant is virus-infected, it remains so for its entire life.

HOW DO ORCHID VIRUSES SPREAD?
Viruses can spread in the following ways:

Mechanical Transmission
Anything that transfers the plant sap from an infected plant to an uninfected plant: cutting tools, human hands and so on.

Vegetative Transmission
In an infected plant the virus appears in nearly all organs. Consequently, plant parts used for vegetative propagation may contain viruses, and hence infected plants may be reproduced.

Pollen/Seed Transmission
Virus particles within the seed tissues lead to production of virus-infected seedlings. The virus may enter the seed from one or both parent plants.

Vector (Insect) Transmission
Insects, in general, are the major group of virus vectors. Fortunately, CyMV, TMV-O and ORSV are not vector-transmitted.

HOW CAN I TELL IF MY ORCHID PLANT IS INFECTED WITH A VIRUS?
When an orchid plant is severely infected, visible symptoms such as ringspots, streaks, necrotic (black) and chlorotic (yellow) mosaic or mottled discolorations appear on leaves and flowers. However, diagnosis of virus infection by visible symptoms alone is not sufficient, as a symptomless plant may be virus-infected.

DOES AN OFFSHOOT FROM AN INFECTED PARENT PLANT STILL CARRY THE VIRUS IF IT HAS NO SYMPTOMS?
Yes, a virus affects most parts of an infected orchid plant.

ARE SEEDS IN PODS ON AN INFECTED PLANT ALSO INFECTED WITH A VIRUS?
Yes, at least in some cases, CyMV has been detected in seeds in pods on an infected plant.

IS SURFACE STERILIZATION OF SEEDS BEFORE SOWING IN A FLASK EFFECTIVE AGAINST VIRUS?
No, because the virus particles are located within the seed tissues.

CAN MICROCLONING BE CARRIED OUT WITH VIRUS-INFECTED PLANTS?
Yes. However the virus must be eradicated through chemical (viricide) and/or heat treatment during the micropropagation process.

CAN PLANTS BE TESTED FOR SUSPECTED VIRUS INFECTION?
With modern plant protection technology, such as Enzyme Linked Immuno-absorbent Assay (ELIZA) or other laboratory techniques, agricultural or horticultural laboratories can screen orchid plants for suspected viruses. The diagnostic service is available to all growers.

FUNGAL AND BACTERIAL DISEASES

Fungi and bacteria commonly affect orchid plants, most usually by causing some form of rot, or discoloration and spotting of flowers or leaves. A fungus is a mould-like organism which infects a plant and becomes visible when it produces its spores. Bacteria are always far too small to be seen, though the symptoms are visible when the plant becomes diseased. Although biologically speaking fungi and bacteria are very different, they are both treated similarly where orchids are concerned, and often occur together, which is why they are treated together here.

The common symptoms that are attributable to fungal and bacterial attack are rotting, where the plant tissues become discoloured and damp as they die back; discoloration of otherwise living plant tissues, such as streaks or spots of discoloration on leaves or flowers; drying up and general failure to thrive; and moulds, where an encrustation or layer of mould covers parts of the plant.

Rotting can occur in a number of forms, as there are many different bacteria or fungi that can cause it. For example, rot may occur in the apex or crown of the plant where the new

leaves form (crown rot); in the roots and stems (black rot, root rot); or as rotting spots on leaves (soft rot, bacterial brown spot).

Discoloration likewise can occur in various forms, for instance, small brown or grey spots on flowers (*Botrytis* fungus), or black flecks or streaks on leaves (leaf spot), which can be of many kinds depending on the exact infection. A particularly common source of leaf discoloration is Anthracnose fungal disease, in which the leaf develops brown or black dried areas forming bands or concentric rings as the discoloration spreads.

The principles of treatment are always similar. Remove the affected parts by cutting back to clean tissue; spray or paint cut surfaces with a suitable bactericide and fungicide (see below); and dispose completely of infected materials.

Rots

Bacterial and fungal infections, and in particular rots, typically arise when

Left: Bacterial rot (*Pseudomonas / Phytomonas / Erwinia*).These bacterial infections start where the surface (cuticle) of a leaf may have been damaged. Phalaenopsis plants are especially susceptible if kept exposed to rain or to dripping water. Wet, soggy spots are seen on the leaves, spreading rapidly. The spots are a lightish brown and may appear translucent. The affected leaf tissue breaks down and becomes liquid, and may have a foul smell. Spraying with Physan and Streptomycin sulphate (agricultural antibiotic) or Natriphene gives effective control, but all infected plant parts must be removed and destroyed; the liquid from the infected leaves will spread the disease. Less nitrogen (N) and more potassium (K) in fertilizers is helpful, and organic fertilizers should be avoided.

ventilation is poor and humidity is high: if the plants are too crowded, for example, or during rainy weather.

Treatment for all rots is essentially similar. The diseased parts must be cut back to clean tissues, the plants treated with bactericidal and/or fungicidal solutions, all cut surfaces coated with rather concentrated fungicide of the type that leaves a lasting residue, and the plants dried off. In the case of root rots, all dead and infected roots need to be removed, and repotting in fresh potting material done, followed by a less generous programme of watering. Sometimes it is better to leave the plant unpotted in a humid shaded place until new roots appear.

These rots are particularly lethal and quick-spreading amongst seedlings, and can quickly destroy large numbers of young plants if action is not taken

Top Right: *Cypripedium* brown rot (*Erwinia cypripedii*). This is a dry rot affecting Paphiopedilums. The stems and leaves turn a rich brown colour as they die off, starting with small spots. The plant may put out fresh shoots, but these are overtaken by the progress of the disease if not treated. Physan will control the disease.

Right: Basal rot (*Sclerotium rolfsii*). Also known as Southern Blight in America, this is a fungal rot, attacking the crown or roots of the plant. Light brown watery patches may develop at the base of the stem, and spread upwards. White threads of fungus may be seen, with small white or black pinhead sized balls, the fungus fruiting bodies. The whole stem rots and the leaves fall, having rotted at the base. Natriphene or 1% copper sulphate solution can be used for control, and infected plants should be completely soaked in solution after removal of all diseased parts. Captan, Thiram or Zineb fungicides may also be used. In Oncidiums, basal rot is due to the fungus *Mirismiellius*.

Left: Black rot, crown rot, damping off (*Pythium/ Phytophthora*). These are fungal rots, attacking leaves, roots or the crown of the plant. The rot can start as small brown soft spots with yellow margins on the leaves, but if in the crown, the whole leaf appears brownish black and the rot soon extends downwards from the crown.

The leaves of plants affected by *Phytophthora* fungus can often be lifted away from the crown, or may drop out, and the base of an otherwise healthy leaf can be seen to be infected and discoloured black or purplish brown. On cutting back such a plant the stem or pseudobulb may show a similar discoloration. This infected tissue must also be cut out before fungicide treatment is applied. A paste of fungicide can be applied to cut surfaces. The disease often takes a heavy toll of young seedlings (described as damping off). It spreads rapidly once present in a collection. Effective control can be obtained by the use of Etridiazole, Metalaxyl, Thiram, or with most other fungicides.

Note that a type of crown rot is created when excessive sun heats up water contained in the crown of the plant, and kills it. The crown leaves then blacken and die. However, this is a cultural fault and not initially infection.

Centre Left: Damping off in seedlings.

Bottom Left: *Phytophthora* in flower.

---

promptly. Always remove infected plants immediately you find any, as infection spreads rapidly in a collection. Seedlings and also adult plants are more susceptible to rot in wet conditions, especially where the plant is injured. Plants kept outdoors with limited protection from rain are likely to be especially susceptible to rots, and it may be necessary to devise some arrangement for keeping affected plants under shelter until they are properly recovered. It is always best to have seedling plants sheltered from direct rain and dripping water.

Above: Anthracnose (*Gloeosporium*). A leaf spot develops into a large area of dead dry brown tissue with a characteristic concentric banded pattern. The boundary between dead and living tissue is quite abrupt, but often there is a yellow margin. Anthracnose can also attack the flowers, appearing as brownish or blackish raised spots. The infection is quite common, slow-growing and persistent, but can be eradicated by complete removal of infected parts and treatment with fungicide. The infection often develops from dead sunburn patches on leaves. Ferbam, Maneb, Zineb or Thiram, especially mixed with Benomyl, provide effective control.

Top Right: Black leaf spot (*Alternaria, Helminthosporium, Phyllostictina*). Black speckling or spotting is common in many orchids, notably Dendrobiums, and can be a result of a variety of fungi. Generally they are not a serious problem, though the plants are unsightly, and it is often hard to keep plants completely free of spotting. However, a regular regime of prophylactic fungicides (Benomyl, Maneb or Zineb) with removal of infected leaves can achieve good control.

Right: Flower blight, flower rusty spot (*Curvularia, Botrytis*). Several fungi can cause flower blight, with brown speckling or spotting, or falling buds or flowers. *Curvularia* blight or rusty spot causes minute rusty speckles. *Botrytis* attack leaves small grey spots over the flowers. Blights tend to occur when conditions are too damp, with insufficient ventilation. Use of fertilizers with high potassium (K) content may help. Benomyl, Thiram, Ferbam, Maneb or Zineb can be used for control.

Other Fungal Infections

Other orchid fungal infections include sooty mould (*Cladosporium*) and snow mould (*Ptychogaster*). With the former, the affected parts, especially the base of the leaves, are covered with a black deposit. This deposit is persistent, but can be wiped away with some difficulty. The mould causing the condition actually grows on the surface of the plant rather than within its tissues. Insects such as aphids and scale insects secrete sugary solutions which form a growth medium for the mould and encourage it. The eradication of the insect pests is therefore equally as important as

Left: Fusarium wilt. This is a very serious disease which kills plants by inhibiting growth. The roots rot, and water transport within the plant stem is prevented. The plant becomes dehydrated, and even if sufficient water is taken in to maintain the plant alive, it is very slow to resume growth. A general failure to thrive and slow decline of the plant results in its eventual death. A reddish discoloration may be found in infected stem tissues. The buds tend to drop from the inflorescences if any are produced. Control is as for the flower blights. See also *Pellicularia* root rot (page 157).

Left: Cercospora leaf spot (*Pseudocercospora*). This is found commonly in Dendrobium plants. The leaf spotting appears as yellow patches on the upper leaf surface. Subsequently a black deposit of spores is found on the lower surface of the leaf. The leaf eventually dies and falls. In treatment with fungicide, it is important to spray the lower leaf surfaces. Benomyl, Maneb, Zineb or Ferbam are effective for control of the disease.

Bottom Left: Guignardia leaf spot. Black lesions break out on the leaf, forming a streaked pattern. With extensive infection, the streaks come together to form a blackened area, which is rough and scaly. The disease is sometimes confused with *Phyllostictina* (see page 143). As with Anthracnose, the infection spreads slowly, and is persistent, but is treatable by removal of all infected parts and fungicide treatment as for Anthracnose.

eradication of the mould itself, and both fungicides and insecticides need to be used. It is irritating but not a serious threat to the life of the plant. Sooty mould is infecting the plant shown in Chapter Four, page 82.

The snow mould fungus covers the roots with a white encrustation which is not wettable. Therefore the roots so covered become useless. All infected roots should be cut off, and the plant soaked for a time in Physan before repotting. Snow mould is not a common problem.

PESTS

Like other plants, orchids can be damaged by a wide range of pests, most of which are insects. Apart from the damage done by pests such as snails, cockroaches or beetle larvae that actually feed on the plants or their flowers, other pests such as aphids, mites, thrips, or scale insects may infest the plant to such an extent that it becomes seriously debilitated or even killed. A nuisance, but irritating nonetheless, is the depollination of flowers due to the visits of insects, resulting in early flower wilt or even setting of seedpods. Consequently, it is wise to have a preventive regime of pesticides. Infrequent but regular preventive spraying in a healthy collection is more efficient than frequent spraying only when an outbreak of some infestation has occurred. Preventive spraying can also be effective with natural pesticides such as nicotine or derris that are less effective once an infestation has occurred.

The commonest problems are mites, thrips, and scale insects, which tend to overwhelm the plant by heavy infestation; weevils and their larvae, which do damage by boring; and various insects that actually eat the parts of the plant, such as cockroaches, locusts and beetles.

Ants

These are not directly injurious to orchids, but they spread infestations of scale insects, aphids and mealy bugs, and thus indirectly the spread of other diseases. Ants often make nests inside pots, and become rather entrenched in the collection unless steps are taken to deter them. Some commercial insecticide sprays for use in gardens will kill ants, and commercial baits are also available that will destroy ant colonies. Domestic insecticides for use in the home are toxic for plants and should never be used in the garden, but anti-ant deterrent powders can be used on lawns and under shelters.

Aphids

These appear as clusters of small soft-bodied insects sucking sap. They are often green.

Aphids are common garden pests, but they are not usually a severe problem for orchidists. They are common on hibiscus plants. Most insecticides will give control, especially if systemic, and the only damage is if the infestation is very dense, or the injuries give rise to other infections. Aphids have also been thought to transmit virus disease from other plants, but this is uncertain. They are spread by ants, which are attracted by the honeydew they secrete. This secretion also stimulates the growth of sooty mould.

Bees

These and other pollinating insects are a pest if they visit orchid flowers and remove the pollen. This leads to early fading of the flowers. It is almost impossible to prevent this occurring, except by resorting to fine mesh enclosures for particularly prized plants to exclude the bees. This is of course very troublesome and expensive.

Beetles

Various beetles attack orchid plants. In Singapore a yellow beetle (*Lema pectoralis*) is a common pest, especially in Arachnis. The flowers or the root tips are eaten away by the beetle larva, an orange grub. The solitary white eggs laid on the roots or flower stalks can be destroyed by hand. The beetles also feed on the flowers, making irregular holes. Another pest is the beetle *Agonita spathoglottis*, a flat dark-brown beetle about six mm long. The grub carves out a space within an orchid leaf over a nine to ten day period. The affected parts of the leaf dry out as an irregular large whitish patch. The grub pupates inside the leaf, which should therefore be burnt or otherwise destroyed.

It is difficult to prevent attack by beetles completely, but periodic preventive spraying with insecticides such as Trichlorfon, Dimethoate or Diazinon will usually deter them.

Cockroaches
Cockroaches eat the green tips of the roots. As with snails, root tips in or on the potting medium are bitten back to ragged stumps. The cockroaches often live in the pots, and can sometimes be driven out by immersing the whole pot in water for a few minutes. Alternatively, poison baits sold commercially for use with cockroaches can be used. Dipping pots in insecticide solution of Diazinon or Malathion is more effective than spraying, though it is also more troublesome.

Crane Flies
Crane fly maggots can bore holes in Dendrobium pseudobulbs. Treat with systemic insecticides.

Grasshoppers, Locusts
These pests sometimes attack young leaves or flower spikes. They are very difficult to control as they come, inflict their damage, and then leave. Systemic insecticides may deter, but often these pests do some damage even to sprayed plants before moving on.

Mealy Bugs
The bodies of mealy bugs form a white powdery mass around stems and in

Left: Agonita beetle damage to Dendrobium leaves.

Below: Cockroach damage to roots.

protected crannies, such as the junctions of leaves and stems.

Mealy bugs are soft insects related to the scale insects, but larger (up to five mm) and covered in a distinctive white powdery coat. They are incidentally very apt to attack hibiscus shrubs, and are probably more of a pest to the general gardener than to the orchid grower. They can be individually removed with a toothbrush or toothpick, or killed with drops of methylated spirits, if desired. Mealy bugs secrete a honeydew which attracts ants. The waxy body surface protects them from many insecticides, but systemic insecticides such as Malathion are effective. An alternative solution is to spray a dilute white oil emulsion with or without added insecticide. Leaves need to be thoroughly coated when spraying.

Above: Mites on the underside of a leaf.

Mites

Red spider mites and false spider mites are both serious pests of orchids. They attack the leaves and stems, sucking the sap, and can build up to a very extensive infestation that is very debilitating to the plant. They particularly accumulate on the lower surfaces of leaves. The symptom of a mite infestation is a whitish stippled coating on the under surfaces of leaves, showing dirty brown or blackish discoloration and eventual death of leaves. Minute red specks may be visible on the leaf surface, and a reddish discoloration may be found if the surface is wiped with dry tissue paper.

Strictly speaking, mites are arachnids (spider family) not insects, and they are resistant to many insecticides. Control of mites requires the use of acaricides (miticides). Amitraz,

Diazinon, Dimethoate and Propargite are effective for mite control.

Red spider mites are the commonest type of mite. They are minute, under one half mm long, and barely visible to the naked eye, except as minute reddish flecks on the leaf. The whitish discoloration on the undersurface of the leaf is caused by the minute webs of these creatures. The false spider mites are slightly smaller and do not spin webs. Both true and false mites may be red, orange, yellow or greenish. Any mite infestation tends to be described as 'red spider' or 'spider mite' and the treatment is similar in all cases. The mites reproduce by laying eggs, which are not always affected by acaricide treatment, therefore treatment should be repeated at intervals of four to eight days to ensure that all newly hatched mites are also killed.

Spider mites and false spider mites have a reputation in cooler climates for needing a dry environment, being discouraged by high humidity. However, the natural humidity of the tropical lowlands does not seem to pose any deterrent to them, as they are a very common pest. It does not seem feasible to cure an attack of mites by cultural treatment, and acaricide treatment is the only effective one. Since the infestations are worst on the lower leaf surfaces, it is important in spraying to ensure that the spray reaches these surfaces.

Scale Insects

These form more or less dense infections of tiny brown scales covering plant leaves and stems, especially on older parts of the plant. There may be yellowing or discoloration of infested surfaces.

Scale insects cling to the stem or leaf and suck sap. Soft scales look like little brown scales maybe one mm long, hence the name. Soft scale insects may be brought by ants, which are attracted by the honeydew they secrete. This secretion may also encourage the growth of sooty mould (see page 143). Armoured scales are larger, up to three mm, and a darker brown. Both types can multiply to give a heavy infestation. They are not very susceptible to contact poisons, because the waxy scales provide protection; but use of oil-based insecticides can get round this problem.

As with mealy bugs, it is easier to use systemic insecticides, which circulate in the sap and thus readily kill scale insects. Dimethoate or Triazophos provides effective control, but it is less toxic to spray a dilute white oil emulsion with or without some added Malathion. The leaves have to be thoroughly coated.

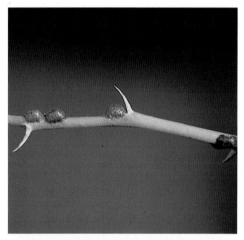

Top Left: Armoured scale insects.

Centre Left: Soft scale insects.

Left: A slug on a leaf.

Slugs and Snails

These are common in many gardens and feed mainly at night. They eat young shoots and root tips. Large species, such as the common giant snail (*Achatina fulica*) can be controlled by hand, but less obtrusive species are better tackled by laying down a metaldehyde bait. Slugs and snails can do damage to roots hidden in pots, and an eye should be kept open for slugs and snails when repotting. A very minute species of snail with a shell only a few millimetres across is sometimes found in potting mixtures, or in fern root slabs, and can only be eradicated by the use of bait or liquid metaldehyde. Snails will not cross dry cotton wool, and a collar of cotton wool applied around an inflorescence will protect the flowers, as long as it stays dry.

Sparrows, Squirrels

Larger creatures such as these can be a problem. They attack young shoots. Insecticides are not much use, and trapping or scaring these creatures can be difficult.

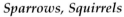

Top Right: Slug damage to flowers.

Right: Squirrel damage.

Below: Snail damage to roots.

Above: Weevil damage.

Top: Thrips damage to flowers.

Thrips

The signs of thrips attack are failure of the flower bud to open, or distortion of the flower with brown patches or uneven coloration, or white streaks.

Thrips are small slender flying insects about one mm in length. They attack orchid flowers, especially in hot, dry spells, feeding on the sap. When thrips are around, weekly spraying is needed, and although fresh attacks can be controlled by contact insecticides, systemic (circulating) insecticides are needed to control thrips hidden in buds.

Effective insecticides include Dimethoate, Diazinon and Triazophos.

Weevils

The main symptoms are holes in pseudobulbs or shoots, especially near the crown. Always suspect weevil damage when the crown of a plant suddenly shows damage, which may then lead to fungal or bacterial infection. Holes in Dendrobium pseudobulbs may also be caused by crane fly maggots.

Weevils are beetle-like insects with long snouts adapted for boring, familiar to anyone whose staple carbohydrate is rice. Several kinds of weevil (e.g. *Orchidophilus aterrimus*) attack orchids by boring holes into the growing shoots, or other parts, and laying their eggs there. These eggs hatch into larvae (white grubs) that feed in on the internal plant tissues. The weevils are small, about five mm long, but are a serious pest as a single attack can easily kill the growing shoot. In Phalaenopsis plants especially this can easily kill the plant, particularly as the damaged tissue is also apt to develop rot or other infection. Weevils also feed on flowers and buds. Weevils seem to like Dendrobium and Phalaenopsis plants in particular. They should always be destroyed at once by hand if seen, but Carbaryl or systemic insecticides are helpful in deterring them. It is also necessary to apply fungicide liberally to damaged crowns, to reduce the chances of secondary infection.

SOME COMMON SYMPTOMS

Diseases

Symptom	*What it might be*
Flowers become spotted with brown speckles	*Botrytis, Curvularia* and other fungi
Flowers show streaking of the colours (colour break)	Genetic defects; virus infection
Flower spray wilts and rots	*Phytophora* fungal infection
Leaves covered in sooty black deposit, especially at the base	Sooty mould
Leaves show heavy black patches or streaks	Virus infection; crown rot or black rot
Leaves show black streaks	Guignardia fungal infection
Leaves show black spotting or freckling	Cercospora, *Phyllostictina*, other fungi; viruses
Leaves show heavy yellow or yellow and black mottled discoloration	Virus infections
Leaves show ring-shaped black or yellow marks	Ring virus
Leaves show brown spots with yellow edges	Bacterial rot; Cercospora fungus
Leaf shows rapidly spreading brown patch of soft tissue	Bacterial rot
Leaf: dry dead part shows regular or concentric bands	Anthracnose fungus
Leaf becomes loose and lifts away, base is rotten	Black rot or crown rot; basal rot
Leaves in crown become brown and rotten	Bacterial rot; black rot/crown rot; damping off
Leaves in crown black, especially at the base, and lift away	Black rot or crown rot
Paphiopedilum leaves turn dark brown and shrivel	Cypripedium brown rot
Plant fails to thrive and leaves/roots appear dessicated	Fusarium wilt
Roots covered in white encrustation, plant dries out	Snow mould
Roots shrivel and rot	Black or basal rot, Fusarium wilt, *Pellicularia*
Shoots or pseudobulbs rot upwards from the base	Basal rot

SOME COMMON SYMPTOMS

Pests

Symptom	What it might be
Flowers show distortion and discoloration, flower spike may be distorted	Thrips
Flower spike may be eaten	Snails; beetles and beetle grubs; caterpillars; grasshoppers and locusts
Flowers eaten	Beetles
Leaves eaten	Snails; locusts; bird damage
Leaf whitish or silvery underneath, with yellow or black discoloration. Minute reddish specks may be visible	Red spider mites; false spider mites
Leaves covered with tiny brown specks that can be scraped off	Scale insects
Leaves eaten away in patches leaving a skin	Agonita beetle
Leaf bases or flower spikes infested with a white powdery mass	Mealy bugs
Root tips eaten away	Cockroaches; snails
Young leaves or pseudobulbs show small holes, small black insects that are hard to crush may be seen	Weevils; crane fly maggots
Young shoots and leaves eaten	Slugs, snails, squirrels, sparrows

Cultural Problems

Symptom	What it might be
Buds drop off before the flowers open	Polluted atmosphere; too much or too little water
Leaves turn yellowish green	Too much sun
Leaves turn wrinkled and dry	Not enough water; atmosphere too dry
Whitish patches of dead tissue form in the middle of leaves	Sunburn: give less direct sun

Symptom	*What it might be*
Plants will not flower again	Plants need repotting; plants too shaded; too much high nitrogen fertilizer; plants needs drying out after growing; imported plant unsuited to lowland tropics
Plants generally fail to thrive	Old potting material; pot too large or too small; failure to fertilize; inadequate or excessive watering; plant diseased

Bottom: Cultural faults: sunscorch. The black dead patch is surrounded by whitish leaf tissue. This white colour is typical of leaf scorching in excessive direct sun.

Below: Cultural faults: sunscorch.

Bottom: Cultural faults: crown rot due to watering in hot sun.

Below: Cultural faults: excessive use of growth hormones has discoloured these leaves.

153

Spraying

PREPARING TO SPRAY

• When several chemicals can be used for a particular purpose, select the least toxic.

• The manufacturer's instructions should be read and followed, especially as regards concentrations.

Above: Spraying an orchid collection with chemicals. It is wise to wear protective clothing at all times when using dangerous substances. This grower should also be wearing gloves.

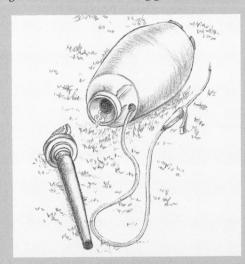

Above: Disposal of surplus chemical solution after use. It should not be poured into a drain, but on to grass, on waste ground or in an out-of-the-way corner of the garden.

• Do not use leaking or faulty spray apparatus.

• Choose a time when chemical odours will not disturb others, and when drifting spray will not be a hazard to passers-by or others in the vicinity.

• Do not mix chemicals unless they are known to be compatible (see manufacturer's label).

• Do not let the chemical come into skin contact. Use disposable gloves. Do not inhale any spray or powder.

• Preferably wear protective clothes, masks and goggles.

WHEN SPRAYING

• Use a fine spray to cover the upper and lower surfaces of the leaves or flower spikes thoroughly. Some fungicides will leave an unsightly deposit on the flower if sprayed when the flower is opened.

• Stand upwind of any spray.

• Do not spray in hot sunlight.

• Never let chemicals at any time come into contact with or near food or drink. Do not smoke, eat or drink while spraying.

• Wash immediately if spillage comes into contact with your skin.

• Stop spraying at once if you feel unwell. Seek medical advice if you do not immediately recover. Take the chemical container or its label with you if seeking medical treatment for suspected poisoning.

• Chemicals are dangerous to animals, especially fish and caged birds, so avoid spraying if there are any nearby.

AFTER SPRAYING

• Rinse out the equipment. Discard residues and surplus on earth rather than in drains. Clean out spray nozzles by spraying with some plain water.

• Wash yourself after spraying. Have your clothes washed also.

• Store all chemicals in a secure place away from food and where children cannot get near them.

• Dispose of empty containers safely and do not keep them for other purposes.

USE OF TOXIC CHEMICAL TREATMENTS

It can be hard to eradicate a disease or pest once it is well established in a collection, so prevention is better than cure. Most growers apply a regular regime of preventive spraying with insecticides, fungicides and acaricides (miticides). These are toxic substances, and spraying is not without its hazards. Careful attention to manufacturers' instructions and the necessary precautions are essential. It is also necessary to consider wind direction and neighbours when spraying.

The most effective pesticides are those that are systemic, that is, they circulate in the sap. They are carried to all parts of the plant, and are not washed off. They are effective against pests that eat the plants, or which suck the sap.

Horticultural toxic chemicals are supplied in concentrated form, making them more hazardous than when diluted. They must therefore be stored securely and handled with care.

Chemicals and Their Names

For any given insecticide, miticide, fungicide or bactericide, there are three different names: the common name; the chemical name; and the trade name or names. For example, a common general action fungicide is Thiram. Thiram is a common name. The chemical name is tetramethyl thiuram disulphide. It is actually supplied under a variety of trade names such as 'Polyram-Ultra', 'Tersan' or 'Tripomol'. In this book the common names are given; they will be given on the manufacturer's label, which should be carefully read before any purchase is made.

Toxicity

Almost all substances used in treating plants for pests or diseases are toxic, some very much so. The LD50 score is used as a rough guide to toxicity. It is the number of milligrams per kilogram of body weight needed to kill 50% of test animals. The lower the score the more toxic the chemical substance.

• Substances scoring below 50 are considered highly toxic, and none are recommended in this book.

• Substances with a score between 50 and 500 are moderately toxic. If used at all, they should be used only to control a severe outbreak, and never for purely preventive purposes.

• Substances with a score of 501 to 5000 are slightly toxic, though they should be used with care since some substances have a cumulative effect.

• Substances with an LD50 score in excess of 5000 are relatively non-toxic, though they should still command care and respect in handling.

Fungicides and Bactericides

A wide range of proprietary preparations is available. Most fungicides can be used prophylactically, and most fungicides are only surface agents. Bacterial rots can also be treated with the application of horticultural antibiotics, such as Agrimycin or Phytomycin. A 1% solution of Copper Sulphate is also effective in cases of basal rot and root rot, as a sterilizing agent. Other sterilizing or disinfecting agents are Natriphene 0.05% or Physan detergent and algicide (algae killer). Physan is just within the moderately toxic range, with an LD50 score of 500, but the other substances listed are at most only slightly toxic.

TABLE OF INSECTICIDES

PESTS	TREATMENTS		
	Relatively Non-toxic	*Slightly Toxic*	*Moderately Toxic*
Ants	Commercial baits as sold for colony eradication; 'anti-ant' dusts sold as deterrents; garden insecticide sprays.		Chlordane, Diazinon
Aphids	Albolineum (white oil)	Malathion	Diazinon, Carbaryl, gamma-BHC, Triazophos, Trichlorphon
Bees	Not applicable		
Beetles	Derris	Malathion	Diazinon, Carbaryl, Dimethoate, Trichlorphon, gamma-BHC, Triazophos
Cockroaches	Commercial baits sold for cockroach control; or submerge the pot to drive resident cockroaches out of hiding.		Diazinon
Mealy Bugs	Albolineum (white oil), with or without added insecticide	Malathion	Diazinon, Dimethoate, Triazophos
Mites	Albolineum (white oil), Tetradifon. Specific miticides are best	Amitraz, Propargite, Cyhexatin	Diazinon, Dimethoate, Dimite
Scale insects	Albolineum (white oil) with or without added insecticide	Malathion	Diazinon, Dimethoate, gamma-BHC, Triazophos
Slugs and Snails		Metaldehyde	
Thrips	Derris	Malathion	Carbaryl, Diazinon, Dimethoate, gamma-BHC, Triazophos
Weevils	Pick by hand. Systemic insecticides may deter.		Carbaryl

LIST OF EFFECTIVE SPECIFIC BACTERICIDES AND FUNGICIDES FOR GIVEN INFECTIONS

INFECTION	TREATMENTS	
	Relatively Non-toxic	*Slightly Toxic*
Anthracnose *Gloeosporium, Colletotrichum*	Benomyl, Maneb, Zineb	Ferbam, Thiram
Bacterial rot *Erwinia, Phytomonas, Pseudomonas*	Streptomycin sulphate (antibiotics) (not for Vandas)	Natriphene, Physan
Basal rot *Mirismiellius, Sclerotium*	Captan, copper sulphate 1% solution, Zineb. NB: Benomyl should NOT be used as it may promote growth of this fungus.	Natriphene, Thiram
Black rot, crown rot, damping off of seedlings *Phytophthora, Pythium*	Benomyl, Captafol, Captan, Zineb	Etridiazole, Metalaxy, Thiram
Black leaf spot *Alternaria, Helminthosporium Phyllostictina*	Benomyl, Captan, Maneb, Trifoline, Zineb	Ferbam, Thiram
Cercospora spot *Cercospora*	Benomyl, Captan, Carbendazim, Maneb, Zineb	Ferbam
Flower blight *Botrytis, Curvularia*	Benomyl, Maneb, Zineb. NB: Avoid use of Captan to spray flowers as it may damage them.	Ferbam, Thiram
Fusarium wilt *Fusarium*	Benomyl: remove infected leaves.	Ferbam, Thiram
Guignardia spot *Guignardia*	Benomyl, Maneb, Zineb	Ferbam, Thiram
Root rot *Pellicularia*	Zineb	Natriphene, Thiram
Sooty mould *Cladosporium*	Benomyl: ensure insect pests, especially ants and scale insects, are also eradicated	Physan (wipe the leaves)

Chapter Eight

Seedling Culture

All new orchid hybrids start from seed. The orchid seed is so tiny that it does not have any reserve of food of the kind that is found in other plant seeds, and in the natural state it survives and germinates only if it becomes infected with a specific fungus. The fungus provides necessary sugars for the survival and germination of the seed. Eventually the growing seed forms chlorophyll and becomes a tiny independent green plantlet.

For many years the only way in which orchid hybrid plantlets could be obtained was by sprinkling the seeds on to a suitable bed of moss or bark in which a culture of the fungus was maintained. However, the essential ingredient of the cycle provided by the fungus was sugar. It was eventually discovered by Dr Lewis Knudson in 1922 that if the seeds were sown on agar jelly containing sugar and essential mineral salts, the seeds would germinate and grow.

To stop unwanted moulds and bacteria growing on the agar, the seeds were sown in sterile flasks and grew in them sealed off from the world, though with provision for ventilation through cotton wool plugs. Later on they were transferred to further flasks, when the medium became exhausted or too crowded as the seeds grew, or to the outside air for growing in the ordinary way.

This procedure became widely practised, and huge numbers of seedlings became available. Many enthusiasts who had no facilities for sowing seed under sterile conditions were nevertheless able to purchase seedlings, either in flasks or in various stages of development after removal from the flasks. It was possible to rear a large number of seedlings in the hope that one or two might turn out to be exceptionally fine. The plants took up space, and patience was also required, for it could take several years for a seedling to reach flowering size after being removed from the flask. But the excitement and commitment of the enthusiasts and commercial nurserymen alike meant that interest turned to how the seedlings should be cared for. Today, many enthusiasts grow from seedlings, which can be purchased in flasks or as minute plantlets from orchid breeders.

Opposite: Rows of *Doritis pulcherrima* growing in an orchid nursery.

GROWING SEEDLINGS

Growing orchid seedlings is not difficult, but they are much more vulnerable than larger plants. The most precarious period in the life of an orchid plant is when it is a seedling, those few months from the time it is first removed from the sterile flask and introduced to the open air. This is when the casualty rate is the highest. However, it need not be so provided certain precautions are taken.

Sometimes one can purchase flasks containing just a few plants, but more often the flask is crowded. If the flask is too crowded but the seedlings are still too tiny to be planted out of flasks, they will need to be re-flasked with fresh agar medium. This is a job best done by a commercial firm specializing in orchid

seedling culture. But if most of the seedlings have leaves over three cm long, they are ready to be removed from the flasks. Before doing so it is recommended that the flasks containing such seedlings be placed gradually in positions of brighter light for two to four weeks. This is to harden the plants. However, make sure that no ray of sun, even in the early morning, shines directly on to the flasks, as they turn into miniature greenhouses and this may cause plant burn.

Most seedlings are cultured in narrow necked conical flasks, jam jars or whisky bottles. These flasks or bottles need not be broken as they can be re-used. Using a hooked wire, or a pair of long forceps with curved ends, the seedlings can be carefully extracted. Tease them apart gently to avoid damage to tender roots and young leaves. The seedlings come out more easily if rinsed with water a few times in the flasks. If the bottle opening is large, for example a jam jar, the seedlings can be shaken out into a basin of water. If you decide to break the flask or bottle, place it first on some old newspaper. Cover the part where you intend to break with a thick piece of rag, or wrap it in old newspaper. Using a hammer, break the bottle with one or two careful blows. In this way there will be no flying splinters. Take care not to cut your fingers or hands when removing the seedlings.

Top Left: After loosening the seedlings by rinsing with water in the flask, cautiously hook them out with a wire.

Left: Rinse the seedlings in running water. A colander will prevent any getting lost down the plughole. They must be handled gently, but be sure all residual agar-agar jelly is washed off as moulds will grow on any left on the seedlings.

WASHING THE SEEDLINGS

Rinse the seedlings thoroughly in a sieve in a basin of water, ensuring that all pieces of agar are completely removed. Have another two or three rinses to make completely sure. Some growers grasp a handful of seedlings at a time and clean them under a running tap. Next, soak the seedlings for a few minutes in a dilute solution of fungicide. Some prefer a solution of fungicide and bactericide combined, for example Natriphene. Others include fertilizer in the mixture as they believe some of the nutrients may be absorbed which will give the seedlings a better start. Always take care when using chemical fertilizers, fungicides or pesticides, even when very diluted. It is better to put on a pair of thin rubber or plastic gloves.

COMMUNITY POT (COMPOT) MEDIA

When first removed from the flasks, most seedlings will be too small for individual pots, being only a few centimetres high. They are therefore generally grown together in community pots (compots). A wide variety of potting media can be used, including fir bark, fern root, osmunda, sphagnum moss, granite chips, coconut fibre, charcoal, bricks, styrofoam and expanded clay (laka). All pots and potting media should be new. If old pots have to be used, they should be soaked thoroughly and scrubbed with a horticultural disinfectant such as Physan to get rid of algae as well as bacteria and fungi.

Each grower has his pet preference. Broken bricks and charcoal, being easily obtainable and easy on the pocket, are the most commonly used in Malaysia and Singapore. Granite chips are used in some nurseries, but demand frequent

Top: The seedlings in these flasks are large enough to be planted out into community pots. The seal of alufoil allows enough gas diffusion to supplement the atmosphere in the flasks. Other growers prefer to plug the flasks with cotton wool.

Above: Growing seedlings without pots at all. This is an ingenious alternative to compots and thumb pots. These seedlings are growing en masse in a mixture of coconut husk and fern root fibres.

watering as they are non-absorbent. The sizes of the pieces to be used depend upon the roots of the seedlings, but are much less than for mature plants. A few larger pieces should be used for the bottom of the pot, followed by smaller sizes to top up.

161

PLACING SEEDLINGS IN COMPOTS

Separate the seedlings according to their sizes, placing seedlings of the same size in each compot. The largest of the seedlings may be placed immediately in individual two and a half cm pots, using the media of your choice. For the remainder, seven and a half or ten cm compots are used.The pots are filled with potting media to just over one cm from the top.

Take three or four seedlings and place them upright close together against a side of the pot. Holding them in position with one hand, take another three or four with the other and stack them against or by the side of the first lot. Repeat the procedure until the entire pot is filled with perhaps 20 or 30 seedlings. The reason for stacking them close together is to stop the seedlings from drying out too quickly. Prepare a label for each community pot. This should give the parentage of the seedlings (unless they are a repeat cross of a known named hybrid), and the dates of sowing (pollination), harvesting and transplanting. As an alternative to labelling, mark the pot itself, when dry, with a water-resistant felt-tipped pen. Many growers use a code number on labels or when marking pots, and keep a separate record of parentage and other details.

LOCATION AND CARE OF COMPOTS

It is best to place the compots in a well ventilated location under subdued light and complete shelter from rain. In this way watering can be controlled.

In the initial stages the compots may be placed close to one another. As the seedlings grow larger to the stage where leaves grow out of the edges of the pots, the compots need to be spaced further apart to allow better air movement around them.

Watering

The frequency of watering should be such as to maintain a balance between keeping the seedlings too moist and preventing them from drying out completely with improved air movement. The important thing is to understand the environmental factors (or microclimate) of the location where the compots are to be placed and adjust your watering and other cultural practices accordingly.

Watering should preferably be done with a fine spray so as not to disturb the seedlings or damage the tender roots. How often to water depends on the location (whether it is under complete or partial shade), and other microclimatic factors: depth of shade, temperature, humidity and air movement. Some growers water twice a day whilst others only once, giving an additional spray when it is very hot or when there is a strong breeze blowing.

It is generally felt that seedlings do better sheltered from the rain. However, many successful growers find they have little choice and still manage to rear the

Left: A freshly planted compot. The pot is 10 cm in diameter.

The Bell Jar Method

Some growers use the bell jar method, which is particularly useful for the tiniest of the seedlings, as the humidity within the jar can be maintained at a constant level. Also, insects, slugs and snails are prevented from getting to the seedlings. Used one-and-a-half or two litre plastic soft drink bottles are ideal for this. The outer portion (about five cm high) which holds the bottom of the bottle is removed by the application of gentle heat, about 60°C. This is used to house the tiny seedlings resting on moist sphagnum moss or other media. The bottle itself is cut in two about halfway down, and the bottom half is inverted to cover the seedling pot like a bell jar. The sphagnum moss or other media used must be kept moist to maintain the humidity within the bell jar. This method also reduces labour as there is no need to water the seedlings as frequently as with open composts.

The bell jar method may be used as an intermediate stage until the seedlings are large enough to be transferred to open composts. If you prefer, let the seedlings grow until they are big enough to go into individual pots.

Above: Using a home-made plastic bell jar to increase humidity. In this example, the jar is used to encourage root growth in Phalaenopsis plantlets sprouting from an old flower spray.

plants well, provided that they pay particular attention to problems of fungal infection. It is best to avoid situations where water drips on to the seedling. The spray obtainable from a garden hose fitting is acceptable, though a watering can with a fine rose on the spout may need to be substituted in the interests of water conservation. Early morning watering is probably best.

For Phalaenopsis, potting media such as lightweight clay aggregates or gravel can be used instead of the usual charcoal, provided the plants are watered twice daily with a fine spray. The seedlings may be protected from dehydration by placing them in a PVC-lined box.

This guarantees a high humidity. However, the tray thus created must have some drainage holes to prevent any mosquito larvae. Shelter from the rain is essential with this method.

There is no necesssity to fertilize seedlings when they are first removed from flasks and transferred to composts, though some growers favour an initial soaking in dilute fertilizer solution. It is more advisable to wait until new roots appear, which will take about three weeks to a month, before applying fertilizer. During this stage the seedlings are very susceptible to fungal rot and bacterial attack. Therefore regular preventive application of fungicide is advisable.

TRANSPLANTING SEEDLINGS INTO THUMB POTS

Seedlings are ready to be transplanted from compots into thumb pots when the roots have outgrown the pots. To remove the community of seedlings, the pot is dipped in water to wet the potting media and all the roots. After a few minutes, the plants can be dislodged by turning the pot sideways and tapping on the bottom. Occasionally it may be necessary to break the pot. Individual seedlings can then be carefully separated from one another and from the potting media. During this process, care must be taken to avoid too much damage to the roots.

Thumb pots used for seedlings are tiny clay or plastic pots, about two and a half cm in diameter. If they are not brand new, which is best, they should be thoroughly cleaned and soaked in Physan. First the pot is half-filled with some one cm pieces of brick or charcoal. One seedling is then placed in the centre of each pot and a layer of charcoal to cover the roots and support the plant in an upright position. After planting, seedlings in the thumb pots are watered. They are placed close together in shade or under a netting allowing 50% sunlight.

GROWING IN THUMB POTS

In the initial stage, the seedlings are watered twice daily. Watering can be reduced to once daily, depending on microclimate, as soon as seedlings are established in the pot with roots growing and binding the potting medium. When the seedlings are transplanted into thumb pots, you may follow a regular fertilizing regime. The seedlings are normally fertilized twice a week and the fertilizer can be combined with a fungicide or insecticide.

Both organic and inorganic fertilizers may be used. For inorganic fertilizers, use one with a balanced N:P:K (nitrogen: phosphorous: potassium) content, or a high N fertilizer since nitrogen is the main component for growth.

Some growers use full strength fertilizers at the recommended frequency. Others use a diluted solution for the first couple of months after removal from flasks before going to full strength. Yet others use a very diluted solution at every watering. All of these growers alternate between an application of organic and inorganic fertilizer. The general rule regarding frequent but dilute fertilization applies here. Not all seedlings are equally tolerant of chemical fertilizers, which should therefore be used with care.

TRANSPLANTING SEEDLINGS TO BIGGER POTS

Usually seedlings will need to be potted on twice from thumb pots, before they

Left: It is sometimes possible to repot a Vandaceous seedling without first removing it from its old pot. This minimizes disturbance to the plant, but should only be done if all the roots are in good condition, requiring no pruning of dead ends.

Control of Fungal and Bacterial Rot

• Casualties among seedlings are usually caused by fungal rot, and bacterial rot. Therefore regular application of fungicide and bactericide is important.

• Fungicides have different chemical compositions and their effectiveness varies with different fungi. It is recommended that different fungicides be used at alternate applications to give better protection.

• Fungicides may also be mixed with fertilizers to be applied at the same time. If an infection is detected, infected plants are best removed immediately.

• Pests are not common among seedlings, though occasionally a compot may be infested with mites. In such cases, spray with a miticide. Slugs and snails can be a problem with seedlings, in which case metaldehyde pellets should be sprinkled around the pots.

reach flowering size. The best containers are perforated clay pots which will provide aeration for the roots. Solid pots or plastic pots conserve more moisture and are suitable in drier sites. Pot size depends on the size of the plant at the time of repotting. Be sure to give provision for the size that the plant is likely to attain in one or two years. The usual pot sizes range from 8 cm to 30 cm. Do not use an excessively large pot for a plant as it may not thrive when overpotted, and the practice is wasteful of space, potting material and chemicals.

Above: This plant is nearing flowering size, and should flower in the pot shown. Note the rapid increase in size of successive pseudobulbs.

The commonest potting medium is a mixture of brick and charcoal, and the general principles of potting apply.

Newly anchored plants require shade, and should be watered twice a day until the roots have developed and anchored the plants securely to the pot. Once the roots have developed, the plant may then be subjected to fertilizer and fungicide or insecticide. The new plant is fertilized twice a week and fungicide or insecticide may be added at the same time. Watering is done once a day and twice on a hot day. The plants are gradually exposed to more sun to encourage better flowering.

There is no one correct method of growing orchids, whether they are seedlings or mature plants. Orchids are very adaptable to a wide range of environmental factors and cultural practices. All experienced growers say that the learning process is a continuous one. The point that they stress again and again is that a person should observe keenly with a critical eye everything he grows. If his plants are not performing as expected or succumb to disease, he should not despair but accept it as a challenge to find out what went wrong and try again with a different approach.

STERILE CULTURE

The use of sterile culture for orchids has extended both to propagation of seeds and to tissue culture. The former is the means by which new hybrids are grown. The latter is used to propagate large numbers of an existing plant, and has revolutionized the market in cut flowers by making valuable new hybrid clones available in commercial quantities comparatively soon after their first discovery.

ORCHIDS FROM SEED

Propagation of orchids by seed is known as sexual reproduction. Because it requires the use of sterile techniques to germinate the seeds in flasks, many amateurs are deterred from attempting it. However, it is possible to achieve sterile culture with some investment in necessary apparatus, and careful attention to sterilization procedures. It is also becoming possible to have one's seed pods germinated in flasks as a commercial service.

Pollination takes place by the placement of pollen on to the stigma of the flower belonging to the same or to a different plant. The latter case is called cross-pollination. This is followed by

fertilization of the ovules in the ovary resulting in the formation of a seed pod. Fertilization is not immediate as orchids require some time for the pollen tube to grow down the column into the ovary, finding the ovules and injecting the gametes (sex cells) to fertilize the embryo. It may take many months for a pod (or capsule) to ripen. Although an orchid capsule may contain millions of embryos, not all the seeds are fertile (viable). Only viable seeds will germinate into seedlings. Cross-pollination helps to improve vigour and variety by creating an entirely new plant. Hybridization occurs when cross-pollination takes place between two different parent plants of different species or genera, thus producing new hybrids. Basically, it aims at combining the best features of each parent plant into the resulting seedlings. The plant bearing the seed pod is known as the mother plant. It is named first when the parentage of a hybrid is given. For example, *Ascocenda* Yip Sum Wah is a cross registered as *Vanda* Pukele x *Ascocentrum curvifolium*, and we know from this that *Vanda* Pukele was the pod parent.

The seeds of orchids are very tiny, and because of their size, they do not have a food supply to nourish themselves during germination. They are produced in large quantities. Orchid seeds require the help of a kind of fungus in order to germinate. The fungal mycorrhiza supplies nutrients to the

Left: Pollinating a Dendrobium flower. The lip of the flower is pressed down to expose the column, seen here from below. The yellow pollinia are being pushed into the stigma near the end of the column.

seeds while the seed provides a home for the fungus in return, thereby maintaining a symbiotic (mutually beneficial) relationship. This relationship is now superseded by the provision of nutrients in artificial sterile culture medium. Today's orchid growers have added a wide range of substances to their culture media to ensure better seed germination and growth. Such media normally consist of the basic nutrients, coconut water, sugar, agar and water.

The two methods of sowing seeds in vitro, depending on the condition of the seed pod harvested, are explained below.

Green Pod Culture

Green pod culture refers to the culture of immature embryo seeds excised from a still green orchid pod. Normally it is recommended as a rough guide that a pod is harvested for use about half the time it takes for the pod to ripen from pollination. Orchid seed pods take between two and twelve months to reach maturity, depending on the genera and type. Knowing the nutritional requirements of seed germination enables us to culture the immature seeds without having to wait until they reach full development. This method mainly reduces time as seedlings are given an earlier start, thereby shortening the time spent from seeds to flower. Seedlings from new crosses can be obtained more rapidly and a higher percentage of germination is assured as compared to orchids grown in the wild. Seeds of complex crosses can be saved as abortion frequently occurs if pods are left to mature. However, to be successful in green pod culture, fertilized ovules

Above: Green seed capsules (pods). Each will contain up to a million minute seeds, and may take anything up to a year to ripen, depending on the parent plant. However, green pod culture allows the unripe but fertilized seeds to be sown on agar medium before the pod has split and while the seeds are therefore uncontaminated by microorganisms from exposure to air.

need to be used. Thus, from the practical point of view, the determination of when fertilization occurs within the pod is important and therefore when to harvest the pod is critical. All seeds from each pod have to be sown at one time as storage of seeds is not possible. The best time to harvest a pod would be when the end starts to turn yellow. The procedures for immature embryo culture are described below.

The residue of floral parts at the apex of the seed pod are cut away. The seed pod is then washed with antiseptic soap and surface sterilized by soaking the whole pod in alcohol solution for about three to five minutes. The duration of soaking varies according to the size of the pod. After this, the pod is passed through a flame to sterilize the surface, and dissected vertically into halves using a sterile blade. This process should be carried out in a laminar flow chamber. The seeds are scraped up and then sown in a flask containing sterile nutrient media made up of Vacin and Went basic salts, tomato juice, coconut, water, sugar, agar and water. The culture is placed under lighting of 1,000–3,000 lux for between 8 and 16 hours at a temperature of 25° Centigrade, plus or minus 2° Centigrade.

After sowing, the seeds will take from one week to six months to germinate. Dendrobium orchids tend to germinate faster than others in about two weeks to three months, while Paphiopedilums may take six months or more. Germinated seeds can later be transferred to a fresh medium consisting of the same initial media components except with the addition of mashed banana. They will then differentiate and

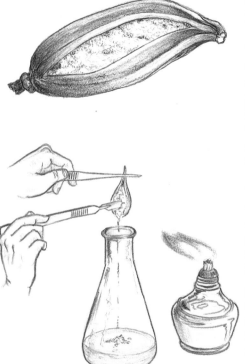

grow into seedlings with shoots and roots. Further transferring of seedlings is made if necessary before they reach the stage when they can be planted out.

Seed Sown Culture
Sometimes the pod is harvested after splitting sets in. Under such a condition, the surface of the burst pod is cleaned with a piece of cotton wool dipped in alcohol. The seeds are then scraped into a conical flask containing 30 ml of 1 to 3.5% chlorox solution and sterilized for eight to ten minutes by shaking. The chlorox solution is then poured away and the seeds rinsed with sterilized distilled water. Lastly, some sterilized distilled water is poured on to the seeds, and they are sown in a sterile culture medium with the aid of a dropper. Subsequent culture is similar to that of green pod culture.

TISSUE CULTURE OF ORCHIDS
Orchids can be propagated by asexual as well as sexual means. Sexual propagation refers to the cultivation of new hybrids, and the plants produced show variation among each other. On the contrary, plants produced asexually, by top cuttings, pseudobulbs, offshoots

---

Top Left: A burst (ripe) capsule, or pod. The seeds will have been infected by air-borne micro-organisms, and they must be sterilized before being transferred into a flask to germinate. Technically, orchid fruits are capsules, but are usually called 'pods'.

Left: Scraping seeds from a green pod directly into the culture medium in the sterile flask. The mouth of the flask will be immediately sterilized in the flame and sealed. The operation is being carried out in a sterile chamber.

Above: Pouring a suspension of sterilized seeds into a flask. As with green pod culture, the flask must then be immediately flamed and sealed.

used for multiplication.

Today, tissue culture techniques are widely used in the cut-flower industry to propagate superior clones of orchids. The process of tissue culture involves the steps outlined below.

Selection of Plant Materials

The mother plant selected should be healthy and free from all micro-organisms. The group of cells used to start the process of orchid tissue culture is known as the explant and the part of the plant from which it is taken is the explant site. In sympodial orchids young side shoots measuring 2.5–7.5 cm should be used. In monopodial orchids, the explant site will be the top 10 cm of the apical shoot. Apical buds or shoot tips and axillary buds can then be obtained from these explant sites. However, this will require the sacrifice of a new growth or even a whole plant in the case of monopodial orchids. Alternative explants such as root tips, leaf tips, flower buds and dormant buds from the inflorescence may be used instead, though success with these sites is limited to only a few genera.

and plantlets, are genetically identical to the mother plant and thus members of a single clone. However, not all orchids produce pseudobulbs, offshoots and plantlets. Besides, the numbers of plants produced vegetatively is limited. Therefore, a new technique, known as tissue culture was introduced by Morel in 1960. Basically, this is a vegetative method of mass propagation of orchids. Actively growing cells or a piece of live tissue are removed from any part of the plant and placed into culturing flasks containing appropriate nutrient media under aseptic conditions. In successful culture, these cells will divide, multiply and differentiate into thousands of plantlets having the same characteristics as the parent plants.

Through tissue culture, a large number of good quality orchids can be produced in a short period. Their products form the basis of the cut-flower trade. The clonal plants are uniform in genetic quality. As tissue culture is not affected by seasonal changes, plants can be produced all year round. It is also possible to produce plantlets free from disease. The mother plant can be tested for the presence of disease before it is

Below: A young side shoot is removed from the parent plant of a sympodial orchid.

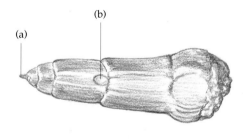

(a)

(b)

Top: The top 10 cm of the apical shoot is removed from the parent plant of a monopodial orchid.

Bottom: The leaves are removed to show the apical bud (a) and the axillary bud (b) on the shoot.

Sterilization

In tissue culture, the presence of bacteria and fungi will prevent the growth of the plant tissue. It is therefore important that the plant material used is thoroughly sterilized and the procedure is carried out in an aseptic environment. A laminar flow cabinet will ensure that filtered air is relatively free from such micro-organisms. Hands must be carefully washed with antiseptic soap and water and wiped with alcohol. All equipment used, such as scalpels and forceps, is also washed with antiseptic soap and dipped in alcohol.

Using a sterile scalpel, the young side shoot is removed from the mother plant. The leaves are carefully peeled off to expose the apical and axillary buds. The exposed stem is then washed with antiseptic soap and water. This stem is later soaked in a 10–12% solution of domestic bleach for five to fifteen minutes. The smaller buds will require a shorter sterilization period, and the bigger apical bud a longer period of sterilization.

Excision and Inoculation

After sterilization, the stem is rinsed with sterile distilled water. With the help of a sterile scalpel and forceps, the bud is excised or cut out from the stem. Care is taken to excise only the bud and not the surrounding tissue.

The excised bud is transferred into a flask containing a sterile liquid nutrient medium, sealed with aluminium foil and placed on an orbital shaker. The liquid nutrient medium is made up of basic salts formulated by Vacin and Went, with the addition of coconut water. The cultured flask is provided with illumination of about 1,000–3,000 lux and shaken for eight to sixteen hours per day at a constant temperature of 25° Centigrade plus or minus 2° Centigrade.

Initiation and Multiplication of Cell Masses (Protocorms)

Shaking during the initial stages is essential for the formation of cell masses on the explant (bud). The purposes of shaking include increasing aeration in the medium, enhancing cell multiplication, and helping distribute nutrients. Depending on the type of hybrids or species, the explant starts to swell after one to two weeks. This further develops into masses of cells known as protocorms in about one to three months' time. They can be multiplied by further cutting into small pieces, which in turn will grow into other protocorms when placed in a fresh liquid nutrient medium. Repeating the same process will enable production of a large number of protocorms.

Differentiation of Protocorms into Plantlets

To encourage differentiation, the protocorms are transferred into a solid Vacin and Went medium with coconut water. After one to three months, shoots and roots will develop. Several transfers into the same medium supplemented with banana and sugar are made before the plantlets are big enough for planting out. As a rule, fast-growing hybrids such as Dendrobiums and Arandas are ready for planting out within one year from the date of first culturing. Slow-growing hybrids such

as Arachnis, Aranthera, Renanthera and Ascocenda may take more than one to two years.

The success of orchid tissue culture depends very much on the stage of explant selected, the sterilization period and the type of culture media used. If the explant is collected at the right stage, this will increase the chances of success in culturing orchids. The time taken to sterilize the explant is vital, as too little will not kill the bacteria and fungi, whereas too much may kill the explant as well. In tissue culture, the type of culture medium used in the initial stage plays an important part. Different types of orchids require different sets of culture media. Improvements and experiments on the various aspects of orchid tissue culture are constantly being carried out to perfect the technique.

Top Right: Cutting away the axillary bud from the shoot. This is done in sterile conditions.

Right: After sterilization in dilute chlorox, the excised bud is placed in a flask containing sterile liquid nutrient. The flask will then be flamed and sealed.

Chapter Nine

Exhibiting Orchids

'A thing of beauty is a joy forever', as the saying goes. As a matter of fact, orchids are potentially almost immortal. Their habit of continual growth means they do not die of old age, only of natural enemies such as disease, accumulated genetic mutations, or neglect on the part of the grower. Having steered the plants past these hazards, the grower feels a natural tendency to want to share the beauty of his or her flowers with others. One feels a sense of achievement when others admire and praise the plants.

SHOW JUDGING

One of the objectives of shows is to promote interest in orchids. You may not feel competitive, or you may have a modest view of your plants, but there is great satisfaction to be gained from submitting a plant that is good enough to obtain an award. And often, after seeing the plants exhibited at a show, you will become aware that your own may not be so far removed from the expected standard after all. Sooner or later most growers are tempted to exhibit their orchids.

At an orchid show, the plants are entered by classes, according to the type of plant. Within each class individual plants are judged against each other, and compete for the prizes. This is

known as show judging. In order to prepare a plant for showing there are various steps to take to ensure it is at its best.

WHAT THE JUDGES LOOK FOR

In show judging, a number of aspects of the plant are taken into account. Rarity and difficulty of cultivation play a part, as does the general plant condition. More important is the overall aesthetic effect of the flower presentation, the quality, size and condition of the flower spike or spikes, and the qualities of the blooms themselves. Aesthetic effects are somewhat subjective, but in general the flowers should be held clear of the plant, and should not be too crowded or too spaced out on the inflorescence. The floral spray itself should not be too old or it may have lost flowers from lower down the spike. If the buds at the very tip of the spike

What to Look for when Showing an Orchid

• The flowers should be spaced out along the spike, and face in different directions in a balanced or regular way.
• The flowers should all be in perfect condition, even at the base of the spike. No pollen should have been lost.
• The flowers should be of good form and size for the orchid type.
• The number of flowers should be high by the standards expected for the type.
• The colours should be pure and in a pleasing contrast.
• The flower substance should be firm and heavy, and the surface texture pleasing.
• The buds at the end of the spike should be fresh and in good condition.

Left: *Ascocenda* Wanpen (*Ascocenda* Pralor x *Vanda* Thananchai).

Below: *Kagawara* Christie Low.

have shrivelled, as they often do, this counts against the plant. The condition of the flowers themselves is also important. They should be free from fungicide deposits, or damage from insects. Because the plants are being judged against others in the same section, the judges look for plants that stand out against other similar plants in terms of the desirable characteristics for that section; but they are not judging the plants closely against the detailed criteria used for award judging (see page 177).

Plant Condition

Although judging centres mainly on the flowers, the plant should also be in good condition. Indeed, exceptionally well grown specimen plants may be eligible for a Certificate of Cultural Commendation under the award judging scheme. A specimen plant is one that has grown to a large size. When in full flower it is an example of what the cultivar is capable of at its best.

As far as possible, a plant in a show should be free of dirty, diseased or blemished stems or leaves. The succession of pseudobulbs should show improving rather than deteriorating growth over the years. Dead leaves and roots should have been removed, and any old flower stalks cut well back. In some shows it is considered necessary or desirable to remove old leaf sheaths and generally to smarten up the plant. Others stress this less, but from the point of view of the spectators a well grown plant attracts attention and

stands out as a testimony to the ability of the grower.

Pot Condition

Early attention given to the potting medium allows the plant to reach peak condition at show time. An old medium may harbour disease and does not promote optimum growth. An appropriate pot size in relation to the size of the plant is important. If repotting is not necessary, then the pot should be scrubbed clean of algae. Plain pots should be used. A decorated pot may not necessarily complement the beauty of the flowers. On the contrary the judge's attention may be drawn away from them.

Right: *Renanthera* Kalsom. The spray is inconspicuously staked with a green stake (see page 176).

Staking of Flower Spikes

Some orchids require a stake or other support in order to show their blooms to their best advantage. Remember that orchid blooms are affected by the direction of the sun. Therefore do not alter the position of the plant unnecessarily by transferring it from place to place, otherwise new and old flowers on a spray may face in different directions, which would not be successful in a show. From an early stage you should train the developing spike so that all the blooms when fully opened will be aesthetically displayed.

Some Phalaenopsis growers, in particular, stake the spray in such a way that it is upright with the flowers arched out at the top. Others prefer to let the spray arch naturally, and this is considerably easier if the plant is growing on its side with the leaves hanging. Oncidiums often have long sprays that can be difficult to manage without staking. Stakes can be made of any convenient material. Stiff wire and fine, green-coloured canes are commonly used by growers. Ties must not be applied tightly lest they damage the growing spike. Plastic twist ties are suitable. The stake should be as inconspicuous as possible.

Light Intensity

Strong sunlight bleaches flower colour very quickly. Greens, yellows and blues fade rapidly in that order. Flowers of these colours should ideally be housed in 70% to 80% shade. Remember that once a flowering plant has been kept for some time in shade to protect the flower colour, it will need to be transferred back to higher light levels cautiously, to avoid sunscorch.

Labelling

Plants should be neatly and clearly but unobtrusively labelled with the correct name, or with the parentage if an unregistered hybrid is entered. Unlabelled plants would not normally be considered for showing. Different shows will have their own provisions for a competing plant to have the owner's name and an identification number recorded in such a way that it is not known to the judges.

Labels come in various materials and shapes and sizes. Plastic labels are the commonest, and may be rigid or flexible. Flexible labels are convenient for hanging plants, as they can be threaded through themselves for easy attachment around a hanging wire. However, they are not long-lasting, being apt to weaken at the neck. Rigid plastic labels are more durable. They can either be inserted into the potting material, or attached to the plant or its pot with a small length of fine wire or plastic string. Tying them on is only possible if they have small hole at one end. Make one with a heated nail if necessary.

Plastic labels take pencil, but indelible ink is better. Most inks bleach with exposure to sun. Some printing inks and laundry pen inks are relatively resistant.

Anodized aluminium is also commonly seen as a material for labels. These labels sometimes carry letters embossed by machine, but this is not practical for the hobby grower. The best anodized labels have a tough surface that takes pencil well and is almost indestructible. The main problem with such labels is that they are apt to become overgrown with algae after a few years, which obscures the name. Plant labels would of course be checked and cleaned or replaced before showing.

PLANNING AHEAD

Having plants for shows is partly a matter of cultural preparation and partly a matter of timing. If plants are maintained in good condition, they can be entered for shows at any time, and the prospect of showing thus encourages good cultural practice. A plant that the owner knows is good can be potted well ahead of show time, so that it will be in peak condition, and this may mean thinking a year or more ahead, but it is no use having a plant in good condition if it flowers at the wrong time. To a large extent, and especially with seasonal plants, the owner is at the mercy of the weather, and cannot do much to control the timing of flowering. However, some degree of control is possible. Techniques such as drying out seasonal plants; nocturnal cooling with ice cubes on the roots, or air-conditioning of plants such as Phalaenopsis which initiate spikes after cool nights; and repotting and applying fertilizers in ways that will help schedule flowering around showtime are all possible. However, you have to know your plants well to be able to exercise these types of control effectively. This means preferably keeping a written record of flowering and growth patterns.

Show Schedule

Take note of the show dates well in advance. Details of orchid shows should be available from the secretary of your local orchid society, together with information on procedure and the classes of plants exhibited. Plan the

Above: Last minute adjustments before a show.

likely plants you wish to enter for the contest. Be accurate with the correct section and class. It is a costly mistake to place a potential winner in the wrong section or class. Some classes permit more than one plant to be grown in a container. If you have surplus plants for individual entries, you can enter them as collections or groups. For such group displays, foliage plants can harmonize well with the orchids, if the show rules permit their inclusion.

AWARD JUDGING

Whether in a show or not, a plant may also be submitted for award judging. Award judging is not unlike show judging, but the criteria are more formal and the standard expected is much higher. In award judging, plants are judged against a set of standard criteria rather than relative to other plants on show. Thus award judging may take place at a show or it may take place at other times. The owner of an award winning plant is privileged to give a varietal name to the awarded plant.

Above *Vascostylis* Tham Yuen Hai

This name will be carried by all plants grown vegetatively by cutting or division from the parent plant, that is, by all plants of the clone. The plant also carries after its name the letters denoting the award.

Award judging serves the purpose of setting and enhancing standards for hybridization, since to gain an award a plant has to be as good as or better than those that have previously been judged and awarded by that society. Once an award is given, the plant concerned and all of its clones carry the initials of the award and the awarding society, according to the guidelines established by the International Orchid Commission (IOC). It therefore sets a public benchmark of quality control, and marks the achievement of both the originator and the grower.

Awards are given in judging sessions, which may or may not be at a show. Often a plant is judged at a monthly meeting of a society, or at a session convened for the purpose. In either case judging is a private business with the judges alone involved. The owner or originator of the cross is not present during judging. Judges are experienced society members who are familiar with the standards against which flowers of various types are measured. It is also possible to send cut flowers to be judged. However, though it is the flowers and not the plant that is judged, it is usually necessary for the judges to be satisfied as to the condition of a whole plant before they will accept it for judging.

Award Winning Orchids

Opposite Top Left: *Vanda* Poepoe 'Diana' HCC/OSSEA. This plant was awarded in 1961, but still shows outstanding flower size and purity of colour by the standards expected of terete Vandas.

Opposite Centre Left: *Grammatophyllum scriptum* 'Green Envy' ABM/OSSEA. A good example of a clear green colour variant, also showing a graceful and dense display.

Opposite Bottom Left: *Catasetum pileatum* 'Green Gold' AM/AOC. A fine example of a species plant good enough to win against hybrid competition.

Opposite Top Right: *Phalaenopsis amboinensis* 'Casandra Lim' HCC/OSSEA.

Opposite Bottom Right: *Aranda* Suntan 'Yee Peng' HCC/OSSEA. The shape is very good for an Aranda, and the colour and arrangement of flowers are also striking.

Orchid Awards

Awards are given by a specific orchid society to a specific plant using the following terminology.
• First Class Certificate (FCC). This highly prized award is rarely given by any society, and has never been given, at the time of writing, by OSSEA. It requires a points score of 90% or more on the points scoring system used by OSSEA.
• Award of Merit (AM). This requires a points score of 80% to 89%.
• Highly Commended Certificate (HCC). This is awarded to plants scoring 70% to 79%.

CRITERIA OF FLORAL EXCELLENCE IN AWARD JUDGING

Flowers are judged according to colour (30%), form (30%), spray characteristics (20%) and other characteristics (20%), notably size, substance and texture. In all these criteria, what is expected of the flower depends on what is the standard for the type. For example, round overlapping form is prized among Vanda and Phalaenopsis plants, but among antelope Dendrobiums or Scorpion Orchids, the prized shapes are not rounded, though fuller broader tepals are still generally preferred when they occur.

Colour

In general, colour is prized when it is deep, clear and unusual. When colours are combined or there are colour patterns, they should not clash. Novelty in colour combinations or patterns is always sought by judges. To some extent, as in other questions of aesthetic quality, the prevailing standards are a matter of taste and convention. For example, it has been customary to award Dendrobiums on the basis of clear deep colours, but flowers with

---

Top Left: *Vascostylis* Blue Haze 'Shavin' HCC/OSSEA. Only the better of the two sprays would have been selected for the judges to consider. The length and elegance of the sprays contributed to the success of this plant.

Centre Left: *Phalaenopsis amboinensis* HCC/OSSEA. Heavy flower texture, good form, and colour contrast and pattern are all strengths of this plant.

Left: *Dendrobium* Laili Fareed. The elegant arching spray displays the flowers well. Deep mauve colour has always been sought after in Dendrobiums, especially combined with rounded flowers.

Top Left: *Vanda dearei* 'Orchidwood' HCC/OSSEA. An outstanding form for a strap-leaved Vanda species.

Above: Near perfection of form in a white Phalaenopsis. Lacking a name, however, it could not win an award, even if its spray were longer.

Top Right: A striking display of Paphiopedilum flowers.

---

blushing tepals have been sought after in recent years. The lip has often been the target of the breeder's attentions, and contrasting or spectacular lip coloration is well regarded in judging.

Form
Form in orchid flowers is very variable. In orchids with broad tepals that present the colouring clearly, the trend in breeding has been to the enhancement of form in the direction of flatter, more open and rounder flowers. In flowers which have other forms, the aim is to reflect and enhance striking, elegant or characteristic forms. An element of subjectivity of judgment is bound to be involved, as to what currently represents enhancement of form.

Arrangement of Flowers
The spray is important as the means by which the blooms are presented. Even in plants with only a single flower at a time, such as some Cattleyas, attention is given to the spray as the means by which the plant displays its flowers. Generally the flowers should be held

181

Above: *Mokara* Esmaco. This is a very good shape, with rounded overlapping tepals and a flat flower.

clear of the plant, on an arching or erect (but not too stiff) inflorescence. The arrangement of flowers along the spray is important, and a branching spray is often regarded as the best. Flowers may be arranged in rows along the spray, which is usually best for Phalaenopsis or arching Dendrobium sprays; or in different directions around it, for Aranda and Vanda sprays, or spread out in a plane, as with many Oncidiums and Renantheras. The flowers should not be crowded together, or spaced too far apart, and the flower colour should not be fading on the flowers that opened earliest on the spray. Generally a spray that is about 70% open is best for judging.

Texture, Substance and Size
Orchid growers pay a lot of attention to the texture and substance of flowers, and this is taken into account in judging. Substance in a flower refers to its fleshiness. A flower of good substance has firm solid tepals, rather than thin papery ones. Texture refers to whether the surface is smooth, shiny, matt and so on.

While larger blooms than usual are often thought desirable, this should not be at the expense of shape and balance, and the overall effect is important. Size is always relative to what is usual for flowers of the kind being judged.

OTHER AWARDS
Besides the FCC, AM and HCC, a number of other awards are given. Two are relatively common: the Award of Botanical Merit (ABM), for species plants that may not be of horticultural merit on account of their small flowers; and the Certificate of Cultural Commendation (CCC), for particularly well grown free-flowering plants.

The system of award judging is commercially important. A plant gains greatly in value as a parent if it carries an award, because the standards maintained by the more prestigious societies are very high, and only definitely superior plants gain any awards. The standards keep rising, since a plant that is awarded will have to be better than those that have gone before. In general the standard of judging for awards is highest in the oldest established societies, in particular the Royal Horticultural Society (RHS), which is the oldest, the American Orchid Society (AOS), the Hawaiian Orchid Society (HOS), the Deutsche Orchideen Gesellschaft (German Orchid Society, DOG), the Société Française d'Orchidophile (French Orchid-lovers' Society, SFO), the Royal Horticultural Society of Thailand (RHT), the Japan Orchid Society (JOS), the Taiwan Orchid Society (TOS), and the Australian Orchid Council (AOC). OSSEA has been giving awards since 1958, but has never given an FCC, evidently maintaining high standards.

Above: Displays like this one are the culmination of months of care and preparation. They leave a lasting impression on visitors and growers alike.

Right: A prize-winning Renantanda, *Renantanda* Azimah AM/OSSEA.

Below: An Ascocenda. The colour contrast and pattern is unusual in Ascocendas. Unfortunately, the spray is too short, the flowers are too small, and the shape is nothing special.

Glossary

Acaricide	A chemical preparation to kill mites, also known as a miticide.
Aerial roots	Roots growing freely in the air.
Agar	A substance made from seaweed which is used to prepare agar-agar jelly for human consumption. It is also used for the laboratory culture of orchid seeds on sterile nutrient jelly.
Anak	The Malay word for 'child', used by South East Asian orchid growers to mean a plantlet growing on its parent plant. Another term is keiki.
Anther	The part of the flower which bears the pollen.
Anther cap	A cap covering the pollen in most orchid flowers, at the tip of the column.
Apex	The growing part of a shoot, in the crown, where the new leaves form.
Apical	At the apex.
Apical Bud	The growth point in the apex of a shoot.
Axil	The junction of the leaf and the stem.
Axillary Bud	A bud on the stem of the axil.
Bacteria	Microscopic one-celled organisms, some of which cause diseases.
Basal	At the base of (the pseudobulb); referring to rot or inflorescence.
Bifoliate	Having two leaves (per pseudobulb).
Bigeneric	Having two genera in its parentage.
Botanicals	This refers to species plants with small flowers of little horticultural interest.
Bract	The scale or leaf-like rudiment where the flower stalk joins the inflorescence.
Bud drop	The wilting or death of buds before opening.
Cane Dendrobiums	The cane-like pseudobulbs of the antelope Dendrobiums (those in section Spatulata).
Capsule	The correct botanical name for an orchid seed pod.
Chlorotic	Showing a lack of chlorophyll, and hence a lack of green colour on a leaf or stem. Chlorotic tissue is usually yellow or whitish.
Chromosome	The thread-like structure that carries the genetic code in a cell.
Clone	A set of genetically identical plants, originating from a single plant by cuttings or mericloning, rather than from seed. The word 'clone' also refers to a single plant which is one of a clone.
Colour Break	An abnormal irregular streaked pattern of colour in flowers, often indicating a virus infection or genetic defect.
Column	The central structure in an orchid flower, bearing the stigma and the anther.
Compot	A community pot: a pot containing a number of seedlings grown together.
Conduplicate	Leaves which are V-shaped in cross-section, as if folded together along the centre line.
Cross	A hybrid (noun); to hybridize (verb), that is to fertilize a flower with pollen taken from a flower of a different species or hybrid.
Cross-pollination	Any pollination in which pollen from one plant fertilizes another, whether or not the two plants are of the same name.
Crown	The leaves at the end of a pseudobulb or stem.
Cuticle	The 'skin' or outer protective layer of cells on a leaf or stem. It is often waxy.
Cultivar	A particular cultivated variety of a species or hybrid.

Cultivar epithet	A name given to an awarded plant and others propagated vegetatively from that plant.
Damping off	A rot affecting seedlings.
Deciduous	Shedding leaves seasonally.
Diploid	Possessing two sets of chromosomes. This is the normal case.
Dormant	Not in active growth; referring to potential growth points.
Embryo	The living tissue in the seed which will develop into a plantlet after fertilization.
Epiphytic	Growing anchored on trees or other plants rather than the ground, but not parasitically.
Explant	Bud tissue (meristem tissue) used in mericloning.
Explant site	The part of the parent plant containing the explant to be used in mericloning.
Eye	A dormant bud.
Flower spike	The growing inflorescence or stalk that will bear the flowers.
Foliar feeding	Application of fertilizer directly to the leaf surfaces by means of a spray.
Fungus	A class of living plant-like organisms, including mushrooms and moulds, that lack chlorophyll, and some of which attack living orchids as parasites. They reproduce by minute dust-like spores, and flourish in damp conditions.
Gamete	Reproductive cells (pollen cells, ovules).
Genera	Plural of genus.
Generic	Of a genus.
Genus	A level of classification one higher than species. A genus contains one or more similar species. The first term of the name in an orchid is the name of its genus.
Grex	A hybrid.
Haploid	Containing only one set of chromosomes: this is the condition of the gametes. The fusion of two haploid gametes in fertilization is needed to create a diploid plant.
Hardening off	Making a plant more hardy, usually by increasing its tolerance of sunlight through gradually increased exposure.
Hirsute	Covered in hairs.
Humus	The organic matter in soil, mainly from decayed leaves and plant remains after bacterial action.
Hybrid	An artificial plant or animal having more than one species in the parent lineage. Most hybrids are a result of human intervention; a few occur in nature (natural hybrids).
Inflorescence	The part of a plant that bears the flowers. The entire flower spike.
Keiki	See Anak.
Labellum	The scientific name for the lip of the orchid flower.

Lateral	Growing from the side rather than from the tip.
LD50	Lethal Dose 50. The dose of a chemical substance sufficient to kill 50% of animals in a laboratory test. A controversial but widely used standard for assessing the relative toxicity of pesticides and fungicides.
Lip	A modified petal, below the column of the flower.
Lithophytic	Growing on rocks.
Marmorate	Mottled.
Mentum	The 'chin', a spur or pouch formed in some orchids at the base of the column where it joins the inner edges of the lateral sepals.
Mericlone	A clone of plants grown from meristem (bud) tissue.
Mericloning	The process of producing mericlone plants under sterile conditions.
Meristem	Undifferentiated tissue, where active cell division takes place, at the growing tips of roots, buds or young leaves. Meristem tissue is the tissue used in meristem culture, for mericloning plants from a single parent.
Micropropagation	Meristem propagation in sterile conditions, giving large numbers of minute protocorms from bud tissue.
Miticide	A chemical preparation to kill mites.
Monopodial	Growing as a single stem indefinitely.
Multigeneric	Having many genera in the parentage.
Necrotic	Dead, referring to a patch or area of tissue.
Osmunda	A type of fern yielding a soft, spongy absorbent root much used in temperate countries for potting orchids, but not commonly used in the tropics.
Ovule	Female reproductive cell (gamete). The unfertilized seed.
Pannicle	An inflorescence with branches.
Pendent	Hanging down.
Pendulous	Hanging down limply.
Petal	A coloured floral part, one of three in an orchid flower.
Photosynthesis	The manufacture of carbohydrates from carbon dioxide gas in plant tissue, using chlorophyll in the presence of light.
Plantlet	A baby plant or seedling.
Plicate	Referring to leaves that are membranous and with many longitudinal folds (the opposite of conduplicate, see above).
Pod	The usual term for a seed capsule.
Pollen	Male reproductive cells (gametes) in higher plants.
Pollinia	The pollen masses of an orchid.
Polyploid	Having more than two sets of chromosomes. Polyploid plants are usually larger and more robust than other plants, with correspondingly larger leaves.
Primary hybrid	A first generation hybrid, one in which both parents are species.
Protocorm	The swollen green germinated orchid seed prior to production of leaves; the mass of cells formed during meristem propagation as a precursor to plantlets.
Pseudobulb	The fleshy bulb-like stem of many sympodial orchids.
Quarter-terete	A channelled fleshy leaf, generally a result of a terete-leaved plant in the recent parentage of a hybrid.

Raceme	An inflorescence without branches.
Raft	A slab of tree fern root or other material suitable for growing epiphytes on.
Repeat cross	A hybrid of the same parentage as one previously made, usually using different individual parent plants.
Rhizome	The creeping, rooting stem between successive pseudobulbs in some orchids (Bulbophyllum, for example).
Saprophytic	Lacking chlorophyll and deriving nourishment from decayed organic matter. Fungi are saprophytic, as are a few little-known orchids.
Semi-terete	A deeply channelled leaf, usually the result of a cross between a terete and a flat or strap-leaved plant.
Sepal	One of three outer floral parts, similar to the petals, but outside them (i.e. the outermost whorl of floral parts).
Sheath	The base part of the leaf that sheaths the stem or the pseudobulb; the membranous sheath surrounding the young flower spike in Cattleya alliance plants.
Species	A group of plants or animals of a single type forming a natural breeding group. The basic unit of classification of plants and animals in taxonomy.
Sphagnum moss	A type of moss with good water-retaining properties.
Spur	An extension of the lip base behind the mentum, containing the nectar.
Staminode	A sterile stamen, lacking pollen.
Stigma	Part of the flower that receives the pollen from another flower, in orchids usually a sticky hollow under the column.
Strap-leaved	Having long curved leaves of uniform width, usually referring to Arachnis tribe or epiphytic Vandaceous orchids.
Sympodial	Growing as a succession of shoots or pseudobulbs.
Synsepalum	The fused (joined) lateral sepals of Paphiopedilums.
Tepal	Collective term for petals and sepals.
Terete	Of leaves, cylindrical; of orchids, having terete leaves.
Terrestrial	Ground-living.
Tetraploid	Having four sets of chromosomes instead of the usual two (diploid).
Tree fern	A terrestrial tree-like fern, the roots of which form a durable, brittle but absorbent mass on which epiphytic orchids can be grown.
Tribe	A group of related genera (e.g. the Vanda-Arachnis tribe).
Trigeneric	Having three genera in the parentage.
Triploid	Having three sets of chromosomes instead of the usual two (diploid).
Unifoliate	Having a single leaf per pseudobulb.
Variety	A species or hybrid variety distinct enough to have a varietal name.
Velamen	The absorbent outer skin of cells in the roots of epiphytic orchids.
Viricide	A chemical to kill viruses on cutters and tools. No viricides effective in killing viruses within an infected plant are known.
Virus	Submicroscopic infectious disease particles made of ribonucleic acid (RNA) or deoxyribonucleic acid (DNA) surrounded by proteins.
Water stress	The physiological effects of lack of water.

Bibliography

Addison, G., *Malayan Orchid Hybrids — First Supplement*, Government Printing Office, Singapore, 1961.

American Orchid Society, *Handbook on Judging and Exhibition*, Florida.

American Orchid Society, *Handbook on Orchid Culture*, Florida, 1988.

American Orchid Society, *Handbook on Orchid Pests and Diseases*, Florida, 1986.

American Orchid Society Bulletin, *Growing Orchids Indoors*, Florida.

Bechtel, H., Cribb, P. J., and Launert, E., *The Manual of Cultivated Orchid Species*, Blandford Press, Poole, UK, 1981.

Brooklyn Botanic Garden, *Handbook on Orchids*, New York, 1974.

Chuo, S. K., *Common Pests of Orchids in Singapore*, Agriculture Handbook No. 4, Primary Production Department, Singapore, 1979.

Comber, J. B., *Wayside Orchids of Southeast Asia*, Heinemann Educational Books (Asia) Ltd., Petaling Jaya, Malaysia, 1981.

Cribb, P. J., *The Genus Paphiopedilum*, Kew Magazine Monograph Series, HMSO/Kew Bulletin, Royal Botanic Gardens, Kew, UK, 1987.

Cribb, P. J., *A Revision of the Antelope and 'Latourea' Dendrobiums*, HMSO/Kew Bulletin, Royal Botanic Gardens, Kew, UK, 1986.

Dillan, G. W., 'Dendrobiums', in *Beginner's Handbook*, American Orchid Society Inc., Florida,1981.

Henderson, M. R., and Addison, G., *Malayan Orchid Hybrids*, Government Printing Office, Singapore, 1961.

Holttum, R. E., *Flora of Malaya, Vol. 1 — Orchids* (third edition), Government Printing Office, Singapore, 1964.

International Orchid Commission, *Handbook on Orchid Nomenclature and Registration* (third edition), London , 1985.

Kamemoto, H. and Sagarik, R., *Beautiful Thai Orchid Species*, Orchid Society of Thailand, Bangkok, 1975.

Knees, S. G., 'Import and Export of Orchids and the Law', in *Modern Methods in Orchid Conservation*, Pritchard, H. W., (Ed.), Cambridge University Press.

Koay, S. H., *Cultivation of Orchids*, Agriculture Handbook No. 7, Primary Production Department, Singapore, 1984.

Koay, S. H., Loi, J. S., and Lam-Chan, L.T., *Cultivated Tropical Orchids*, Agriculture Handbook No. 8, Primary Production Department, Singapore, 1989.

Lee, C. K., *Orchids* (revised edition), Eastern Universities Press (M) Sdn. Bhd., Singapore, 1983.

Morrison, G. C., *The Orchid Grower's Manual*, Kangaroo Press Pty Ltd, New South Wales, 1988.

Noble, M., *You Can Grow Cattleya Orchids*, Mary Noble McQuerry, 5700 W. Salerno Rd, Jacksonville, FL 32210, USA, 1968.

Noble, M., *You Can Grow Phalaenopsis Orchids*, published by the author: 3033 Riverside Avenue, Jacksonville, FL 32205, USA, 1972.

Northen, R. T., *Home Orchid Growing*, (third edition), Van Nostrand Reinhold, New York, 1970.

Northen, R. T., *Miniature Orchids*, Van Nostrand Reinhold, New York, 1980.

Peterson, R., *Orchid Culture under Lights*, Indoor Light Gardening Society of America Inc., New York, 1981.

Phang, V. P. E., *A List of Orchid Hybrids of Singapore and Malaysia, 1960–1980,* Singapore University Press, 1983.

Royal Horticultural Society, *Sander's List of Orchid Hybrids: Addendum 1961–1970*, London, 1972.

Royal Horticultural Society, *Sander's List of Orchid Hybrids: Addendum 1971–1975*, London, 1977.

Royal Horticultural Society, *Sander's List of Orchid Hybrids: Addendum 1976–1980*, London, 1981.

Royal Horticultural Society, *Sander's List of Orchid Hybrids: Addendum 1981–1985,* London, 1986.

Royal Horticultural Society, *Sander's List of Orchid Hybrids: Addendum 1986–1990,* London, 1991.

Sander, David F., *David Sander's One-table List of Orchid Hybrids (1946–60)* (in two volumes), David Sander's Orchids Ltd., East Grinstead, Sussex, UK, 1961.

Sanders (St. Albans) Ltd., *Sander's Complete List of Orchid Hybrids*, St. Albans, UK, 1947.

Sanderson, F. R. and Yong, T. A., *Diseases of Orchids in Singapore*, Agriculture Handbook No. 1, Primary Production Department, Singapore, 1972.

Seidenfaden, G., and Wood, J. J., *Orchids of Peninsular Malaysia and Singapore*, Olsen and Olsen, Freidensburg/Royal Botanic Gardens, Kew/Botanic Gardens, Singapore, 1993.

Sweet, H. R., *The Genus Phalaenopsis*, The Orchid Digest, Inc., USA, 1980.

Teo, C. K. H., *Native Orchids of Peninsula Malaysia*, Times Books International, Singapore, 1985.

Teo, C. K. H., *Orchids for Tropical Gardens*, FEP Internation Sdn. Bhd., Kuala Lumpur, 1979.

Teo, C. K. H., *Tropical Orchid Hybrids*, FEP International Sdn. Bhd, Kuala Lumpur, 1981.

Teoh, E. S. (Ed.), *Orchids: Commemorating the Golden Anniversary of the Orchid Society of South East Asia*, Times Periodicals, Singapore, 1978.

Teoh, E. S., *Orchids of Asia*, Times Books International, Singapore, 1989.

Yong, H. S., *Orchid Portraits*, Tropical Press Sdn. Bhd, Kuala Lumpur, 1990.

PERIODICALS

American Orchid Society Bulletin, American Orchid Society Inc., 6000 South Olive Avenue, West Palm Beach, FL 33405, USA.

Australian Orchid Review, Harbour Press, P. O. Box M 60, Sydney Mail Exchange, NSW 2012, Australia.

Malayan Orchid Review (A Journal of the Orchid Society of South East Asia, Singapore), OSSEA, P.O.Box 2363, Singapore.

The Orchid Digest, P. O. Box 916, Carmichael, CA 95608, USA.

The Orchid Review, 5 Orchid Avenue, Kingsteignton, Newton Abbot, Devon, TQ12 3HG, England.

Registering an Orchid Hybrid

The Royal Horticultural Society, London, is the International Registration Authority for Orchid Hybrids. Only new hybrids (grexes) are registrable. Repeat crosses, selfings, or sibling crosses within a grex are not eligible. This means that once registered, the registered name is applicable to all plants of the same parentage whether from the same or any other pollination, regardless of which cultivar or variety may have been used, and no other name will be accepted subsequently.

Applications to register a hybrid have to be made on the appropriate form, obtainable from The Registrar of Orchid Hybrids, The Royal Horticultural Society, Vincent Square, London, SW1P 2PE, England. A registration fee is payable, £7.50 at the time of writing. It is also possible to obtain forms in Bahasa Malaysia, Chinese, and Tagalog from the Singapore Botanic Gardens. However, the forms must be completed in English. The registrant will need to declare the details of the parentage of the hybrid it is proposed to name, and the parents must themselves be registered hybrids, if they are not species. A description of the flowers should also be given. The registrant need not be the originator of the cross, but if he or she is not, the permission of the originator has to be obtained. Registration of the new hybrid follows a period of scrutiny and checking by the Registrar's office.

There are restrictions on the length of names that can be registered for new hybrids. A new name (a "grex epithet") may not contain punctuation marks or asterisks, and will be regarded as of excessive length if it is:

(i) over 8 syllables and 20 letters overall, or

(ii) over 10 syllables overall regardless of letters, or

(iii) over 24 letters overall regardless of syllables, or

(iv) comprised of over 15 letters in any one word unless it is or is part of a proper noun (e.g. a personal or place name which would appear with a capital initial letter in ordinary prose).

Fuller details are given in the *Handbook on Orchid Nomenclature and Registration*, published by the International Orchid Commission, currently in its third edition: however, a new edition will become available at the 1993 World Orchid Conference in Glasgow, UK. A number of leaflets giving guidance on registration requirements are available from the Registrar, including *OR/G3 Rules for the Formulation of New Intergeneric Names*, and *OR/G6 Special Precautions to be Observed by Those who Propose (in the same Genus) a Series of Grex Epithets starting with the Same Word*.

All the accepted registered names are published in the periodic supplements to *Sander's Lists of Orchid Hybrids*, published at intervals by the Royal Horticultural Society. However, the complete *Sander's Listing* is now also available on compact disc as a computer (PC) database. The new system is called the *RHS Orchid Information System*. It also includes listings of award winning orchids, which can be viewed in colour on screen. It is a joint venture by the Singapore Botanic Gardens, the Royal Horticultural Society, and the American Orchid Society, and is marketed in Asia through the Singapore Botanic Gardens, Cluny Road, Singapore 1025.

The Convention on International Trade in Endangered Species (CITES)

Once a species becomes extinct, it cannot be recovered. It is permanently lost. Many wild animals and plants worldwide are in danger of extinction as a result of the loss of their habitats or the depredations of hunters or collectors. The problem is exacerbated by international trade in such endangered species. Since 1975, this trade has been regulated by the provisions of the Convention on International Trade in Endangered Species, CITES. All orchid species are covered by the Convention.

Species controlled by regulations made under CITES are listed in appendices to the convention. Appendix 1 lists by name individual species considered to be threatened with extinction. International trade in these species is generally prohibited. In exceptional circumstances, trade may be allowed in cases which are not detrimental to the species' survival (e.g. for research or breeding programmes) and are not for primarily commercial purposes.

Appendix 2 lists species or groups not yet threatened with extinction, but which may become so unless trade is regulated. These species may be traded under licence so long as such trade is not considered by an official Scientific Authority of the exporting country to be detrimental to the survival of the species.

In all cases covered by CITES, including plants artificially propagated, exported or imported plants have to be accompanied by a CITES permit or certificate. **All orchid species are covered by CITES.** In addition, all orchid species or hybrids may require a phytosanitary certificate stating they are free of diseases before they may cross many international boundaries. Enquiries regarding permits and certificates may be directed to the Director, Primary Production Department, Ministry of the Environment, Singapore, or the corresponding authority in other countries.

Nine orchid species and two genera are specifically named in the first CITES Appendix as endangered. In reality, however, a number of other species only covered by CITES Appendix 2 are actually in as great or greater danger, for example *Paphiopedilum sanderianum* or *Phalaenopsis gigantea*, both tropical Asian species. The endangered orchid species and genera in Appendix 1 are listed below, together with their geographical distribution.

Cattleya skinneri	Belize to Venezuela
Cattleya trianiae	Columbia
Didicea cunninghami	Sikkim and Uttar Pradesh
Laelia jongheana	Brazil
Laelia lobata	Brazil
Lycaste virginalis var *alba*	Mexico and Honduras (syn. *L. skinneri*)
Paphiopedilum	All species
Peristeria elata	Costa Rica to Venezuela
Phragmipedium	All species
Renanthera imschootiana	Burma, Manipur and Nagaland
Vanda coerulea	Burma, Thailand, Manipur, Meghalya, Nagaland

TABLE FOR CULTURAL REGIMES

The following table lists a selection of the numerous orchid genera, both natural and hybrids, and indicates briefly their preferred regime. Genera that do not grow in tropical conditions have been excluded. Some genera are included under more than one regime, as the plants vary, and the reader may need to consult Chapters One to Four to determine the likely regime suitable for a particular plant. Also given is the recognized abbreviation of the generic name. The list is a long one, and many of the names it contains are rarely found. However, they are included for completeness.

There are many variations within genera, and a table such as this can serve as a guideline only. When in doubt, give the plant more rather than less shade, and harden it off gradually to higher light levels.

Light shade and full shade correspond roughly to one and two layers of mesh netting respectively.

After each name on the list, the recognized abbreviation is given. A blank indicates that the full name is always used.

B = Bench H = Hanging T = Terrestrial C = Climbing	REGIME							
	Full Sun			Light Shade			Shade	
	C	B	T	B	H	T	H	T
Aeridachnis (Aerdns.)	✓	•	•	•	•	•	•	•
Aerides (Aer.)	✓	•	•	•	✓	•	•	•
Aeridisia (Aersa.)	•	•	•	✓	•	•	•	•
Aeriditis (Aerdts.)	•	•	•	✓	•	•	•	•
Aeridocentrum (Aerctm.)	•	•	•	✓	✓	•	•	•
Aeridochilus (Aerchs.)	•	•	•	✓	✓	•	•	•
Aeridoglossum (Aergm.)	✓	•	•	•	•	•	•	•
Aeridopsis (Aerps.)	•	•	•	✓	•	•	•	•
Aeridovanda (Aerdv.)	✓	✓	•	✓	•	•	•	•
Alexanderara (Alxra.)	•	•	•	•	✓	•	•	•
Aliciara (Alcra.)	•	•	•	✓	✓	•	•	•
Andrewara (Andw.)	•	•	•	✓	✓	•	•	•
Angraecum (Angcm.)	•	•	•	✓	✓	•	•	•
Anoectochilus (Anct.)	•	•	•	•	•	•	•	✓
Anoectomaria (Anctma.)	•	•	•	•	•	•	•	✓
Aracampe (Arcp.)	•	•	•	✓	•	•	•	•
Arachnis (Arach.)	✓	•	•	•	•	•	•	•
Arachnoglossum (Arngm.)	✓	✓	•	•	•	•	•	•
Arachnoglottis (Arngl.)	✓	✓	•	•	•	•	•	•
Arachnopsis (Arnps.)	✓	✓	•	•	•	•	•	•
Arachnostylis (Arnst.)	✓	✓	•	•	•	•	•	•
Aranda	✓	✓	•	•	•	•	•	•
Aranthera (Arnth.)	✓	✓	•	•	•	•	•	•
Arundina	•	•	✓	•	•	•	•	•
Ascandopsis (Ascdps.)	•	•	•	✓	✓	•	•	•
Ascocenda (Ascda.)	•	•	•	✓	✓	•	•	•
Ascocentrum (Asctm.)	•	•	•	✓	✓	•	•	•
Ascofinetia (Ascf.)	•	•	•	✓	✓	•	•	•
Ascoglossum (Ascgm.)	•	✓	•	✓	•	•	•	•

B = Bench H = Hanging T = Terrestrial C = Climbing	REGIME							
	Full Sun			Light Shade			Shade	
	C	B	T	B	H	T	H	T
Asconopsis (Ascps.)	•	✓	•	✓	•	•	•	•
Barkeria (Bark.)	•	•	•	•	✓	•	•	•
Beardara (Bdra.)	•	•	•	•	✓	•	•	•
Bokchoonara (Bkch.)	✓	✓	•	•	•	•	•	•
Bovornara (Bov.)	✓	✓	•	•	•	•	•	•
Brassavola (B.)	•	•	•	✓	✓	•	•	•
Brassia (Brs.)	•	•	•	✓	✓	•	•	•
Brassidium (Brsdm.)	•	•	•	✓	✓	•	•	•
Brassocattleya (Bc.)	•	•	•	✓	✓	•	•	•
Brassoepidendrum (Bepi.)	•	•	•	✓	✓	•	•	•
Brassolaelia (Bl.)	•	•	•	✓	✓	•	•	•
Brassolaeliocattleya (Blc.)	•	•	•	✓	✓	•	•	•
Brassophronitis (Bnts.)	•	•	•	✓	✓	•	•	•
Bromheadia	•	•	✓	•	•	✓	•	•
Broughtonia (Bro.)	•	•	•	✓	✓	•	•	•
Bulbophyllum (Bulb.)	•	•	•	•	•	•	✓	•
Burkillara (Burk.)	✓	✓	•	•	•	•	•	•
Calanthe (Cal.)	•	•	•	•	•	✓	•	✓
Carterara (Ctra.)	•	✓	•	✓	•	•	•	•
Catanoches (Ctnchs.)	•	•	•	•	•	•	✓	•
Catasetum (Ctstm.)	•	•	•	•	•	•	✓	•
Cattkeria	•	•	•	•	✓	•	•	•
Cattleya (C.)	•	•	•	•	✓	•	•	•
Cattleytonia (Ctna.)	•	•	•	•	✓	•	•	•
Charlieara (Charl.)	•	✓	•	✓	•	•	•	•
Chewara (Chew.)	•	•	•	✓	•	•	•	•
Christieara (Chtra.)	•	•	•	✓	•	•	•	•
Chuanyenara (Chnya.)	•	•	•	✓	•	•	•	•
Cirrhopetalum (Cirr.)	•	•	•	•	•	•	✓	•
Cochlioda (Cda.)	•	•	•	•	✓	•	✓	•
Coelogyne (Coel.)	•	•	•	•	✓	•	✓	•
Cycnoches (Cyc.)	•	•	•	•	•	•	✓	•
Cymbidium (Cym.)	•	•	•	✓	✓	✓	•	•
Darwinara (Dar.)	•	•	•	•	✓	•	•	•
Dendrobium (Den.)	•	✓	•	✓	✓	•	•	•
Devereuxara (Dvra.)	•	•	•	✓	✓	•	•	•
Diacattleya (Diaca.)	•	•	•	•	✓	•	•	•
Diacrium (Diacm.)	•	•	•	•	✓	•	•	•
Dialaelia (Dial.)	•	•	•	•	✓	•	•	•
Dialaeliocattleya (Dialc.)	•	•	•	•	✓	•	•	•
Disa	•	•	•	•	•	✓	•	•
Dominyara (Dmya.)	•	•	•	✓	✓	•	•	•
Dorandopsis (Ddps.)	•	•	•	•	✓	•	•	•

B = Bench H = Hanging T = Terrestrial C = Climbing	REGIME							
	Full Sun			Light Shade			Shade	
	C	B	T	B	H	T	H	T
Doricentrum (Dctm.)	•	•	•	•	✓	•	•	•
Doriella (Drlla.)	•	•	•	•	✓	•	•	•
Doriellaeopsis (Dllps.)	•	•	•	•	✓	•	✓	•
Doristylis (Dst.)	•	•	•	•	✓	•	•	•
Doritaenopsis (Dtps.)	•	•	•	•	✓	•	•	•
Doritis (Dor.)	•	•	•	✓	✓	✓	•	•
Dorthera (Dtha.)	•	•	•	✓	•	•	•	•
Dresslerara (Dres.)	•	•	•	✓	•	•	•	•
Edeara (Edr.)	•	✓	•	✓	•	•	•	•
Epicattleya (Epc.)	•	•	•	•	✓	•	•	•
Epidendrum (Epi.)	•	•	•	✓	✓	✓	•	•
Epilaelia (Epl.)	•	•	•	•	✓	•	•	•
Epilaeliocattleya (Eplc.)	•	•	•	•	✓	•	•	•
Epiphronitis (Ephs.)	•	•	•	•	✓	•	•	•
Euanthe	•	•	•	•	✓	•	•	•
Eulophia (Eupha.)	•	•	✓	•	•	✓	•	•
Fujioara (Fjo.)	•	✓	•	✓	•	•	•	•
Gotterara (Gott.)	•	✓	•	✓	•	•	•	•
Grammatocymbidium (Grcym.)	•	•	•	✓	•	•	•	•
Grammatophyllum (Gram.)	•	•	•	✓	✓	•	•	•
Hagerara (Hgra.)	•	•	•	✓	✓	•	•	•
Hasegawaara (Hasgw.)	•	•	•	•	✓	•	•	•
Hausermannara (Haus.)	•	•	•	•	✓	•	•	•
Hawaiiara (Haw.)	•	✓	•	•	•	•	•	•
Hawkinsara (Hknsa.)	•	•	•	•	•	•	✓	•
Himoriara (Hmra.)	•	•	•	•	✓	•	•	•
Holttumara (Holtt.)	•	✓	•	✓	•	•	•	•
Hugofreedara (Hgfda.)	•	•	•	•	✓	•	•	•
Irvingara (Irv.)	✓	✓	•	✓	•	•	•	•
Isaoara (Isr.)	•	•	•	✓	✓	•	•	•
Joannara (Jnna.)	•	✓	•	✓	•	•	•	•
Kagawara (Kgw.)	•	•	•	✓	•	•	•	•
Kingiella (King.)	•	•	•	•	✓	•	•	•
Kirchara (Kir.)	•	•	•	•	✓	•	•	•
Knappara (Knp.)	•	•	•	✓	•	•	•	•
Komkrisara (Kom.)	•	•	•	•	✓	•	✓	•
Laelia (L.)	•	•	•	•	✓	•	•	•
Laeliocatonia (Lctna.)	•	•	•	•	✓	•	•	•
Laeliocattleya (Lc.)	•	•	•	•	✓	•	•	•
Lauara	•	✓	•	✓	•	•	•	•
Laycockara (Lay.)	•	✓	•	✓	•	•	•	•
Leeara	•	✓	•	•	✓	•	•	•
Lewisara (Lwsra.)	•	•	•	•	✓	•	•	•

B = Bench H = Hanging T = Terrestrial C = Climbing	REGIME							
	Full Sun			Light Shade			Shade	
	C	B	T	B	H	T	H	T
Limara (Lim.)	✓	•	•	•	•	•	•	•
Lowara (Low.)	•	•	•	✓	✓	•	•	•
Lowsonara (Lwnra.)	•	•	•	✓	✓	•	•	•
Luisanda (Lsnd.)	•	•	•	•	✓	•	•	•
Luisia (Lsa.)	•	•	•	✓	✓	•	•	•
Lutherara (Luth.)	•	•	•	✓	✓	•	•	•
Lymanara (Lymra.)	•	✓	•	✓	•	•	•	•
Lyonara (Lyon.)	•	•	•	•	✓	•	•	•
Maccoyara (Mcyra.)	•	✓	•	✓	•	•	•	•
Macekara (Maka.)	•	•	•	✓	✓	•	•	•
Macodes (Mac.)	•	•	•	•	•	•	•	✓
Macomaria (Mcmr.)	•	•	•	•	•	•	•	✓
Moirara (Moir.)	•	•	•	✓	✓	•	•	•
Mokara (Mkra.)	•	✓	•	✓	•	•	•	•
Moonara (Mnra.)	•	•	•	•	•	•	✓	•
Mormodes (Morm.)	•	•	•	•	✓	•	•	•
Nakagawara (Nkgwa.)	•	•	•	•	✓	•	•	•
Naugleara (Naug.)	•	✓	•	✓	•	•	•	•
Neofinetia (Neof.)	•	•	•	•	✓	•	•	•
Ngara	•	✓	•	✓	•	•	•	•
Nobleara (Nlra.)	•	✓	•	✓	•	•	•	•
Nonaara (Non.)	•	✓	•	✓	•	•	•	•
Nornahamamotoara (Nhmta.)	•	•	•	✓	✓	•	•	•
Okaara (Oka.)	•	•	•	✓	✓	•	•	•
Oncidium (Onc.)	•	•	•	•	✓	•	•	•
Onoara (Onra.)	•	•	•	✓	✓	•	•	•
Opsisanda (Opsis.)	•	✓	•	✓	•	•	•	•
Opsistylis (Opst.)	•	✓	•	✓	•	•	•	•
Otaara (Otr.)	•	•	•	•	✓	•	•	•
Owensara (Owsr.)	•	•	•	✓	✓	•	•	•
Pantapaara (Pntp.)	•	✓	•	✓	•	•	•	•
Paphiopedilum (Paph.)	•	•	•	•	•	•	•	✓
Paraphalaenopsis	•	•	•	•	•	•	✓	•
Parnataara (Parn.)	•	•	•	✓	•	•	•	•
Paulara (Plra.)	•	•	•	✓	✓	•	•	•
Paulsenara (Plsra.)	•	•	•	✓	•	•	•	•
Pehara (Peh.)	•	✓	•	✓	•	•	•	•
Perreirara (Prra.)	•	•	•	•	✓	•	•	•
Phaiocalanthe (Phcal.)	•	•	•	•	•	✓	•	✓
Phaiocymbidium (Phcym.)	•	•	•	•	•	✓	•	•
Phaius	•	•	•	•	•	✓	•	•
Phalaenopsis (Phal.)	•	•	•	•	•	•	✓	•
Phalaerianda (Phda.)	•	•	•	✓	✓	•	•	•

B = Bench H = Hanging T = Terrestrial C = Climbing	REGIME							
	Full Sun			Light Shade			Shade	
	C	B	T	B	H	T	H	T
Phalandopsis (Phdps.)	•	•	•	•	✓	•	•	•
Phaliella (Phlla.)	•	•	•	•	✓	•	✓	•
Phragmipaphium (Phrphm.)	•	•	•	•	•	•	•	✓
Phragmipedium (Phrag.)	•	•	•	•	•	•	•	✓
Potinara (Pot.)	•	•	•	•	✓	•	•	•
Raganara (Rgn.)	✓	✓	•	✓	•	•	•	•
Ramasamyara (Rmsya.)	•	✓	•	✓	•	•	•	•
Recchara (Recc.)	•	•	•	•	✓	•	•	•
Renades (Rnds.)	•	•	•	✓	•	•	•	•
Renaglottis (Rngl.)	✓	✓	•	✓	•	•	•	•
Renancentrum (Rnctm.)	•	•	•	•	✓	•	•	•
Renanopsis (Rnps.)	✓	✓	•	✓	•	•	•	•
Renanstylis (Rnst.)	•	•	•	✓	✓	•	•	•
Renantanda (Rntda.)	•	•	•	✓	✓	•	•	•
Renanthera (Ren.)	✓	•	•	•	✓	•	•	•
Renanthoglossum (Rngm.)	✓	•	•	•	•	•	•	•
Renanthopsis (Rnthps.)	•	•	•	✓	✓	•	•	•
Rhynchocentrum (Rhctm.)	•	•	•	✓	✓	•	•	•
Rhynchonopsis (Rhnps.)	•	•	•	✓	✓	•	•	•
Rhynchorides (Rhrds.)	•	•	•	✓	✓	•	•	•
Rhynchostylis (Rhy.)	•	•	•	✓	✓	•	•	•
Rhynchovanda (Rhv.)	•	✓	•	✓	✓	•	•	•
Rhyndoropsis (Rhdps.)	•	•	•	•	✓	•	•	•
Richardmuzutaara (Rcmza.)	•	•	•	•	✓	•	•	•
Ridleyara (Ridl.)	✓	✓	•	•	•	•	•	•
Robinara (Rbnra.)	•	✓	•	✓	•	•	•	•
Ronnyara (Rnya.)	•	•	•	✓	✓	•	•	•
Roseara (Rsra.)	•	•	•	•	✓	•	•	•
Rothara (Roth.)	•	•	•	•	✓	•	•	•
Rumrillara (Rlla.)	•	•	•	✓	✓	•	•	•
Sagarikara (Sgka.)	•	✓	•	✓	•	•	•	•
Sappanara (Sapp.)	•	✓	•	✓	•	•	•	•
Sarcocentrum (Srctm.)	•	•	•	•	✓	•	•	•
Sarcochilus (Sarco.)	•	•	•	•	✓	•	•	•
Sarconopsis (Srnps.)	•	•	•	•	✓	•	•	•
Sarcothera (Srth.)	•	•	•	•	✓	•	•	•
Sarcovanda (Srv.)	•	•	•	•	✓	•	•	•
Schombocattleya (Smbc.)	•	•	•	•	✓	•	•	•
Schombolaelia (Smbl.)	•	•	•	•	✓	•	•	•
Schomburgkia (Schom.)	•	•	•	•	✓	•	•	•
Scottara (Sctt.)	•	✓	•	✓	•	•	•	•
Shigeuraara (Shgra.)	•	•	•	•	✓	•	•	•
Sidranara (Sidr.)	•	•	•	•	✓	•	•	•

B = Bench H = Hanging T = Terrestrial C = Climbing	REGIME							
	Full Sun			Light Shade			Shade	
	C	B	T	B	H	T	H	T
Silpaprasertara (Silps.)	•	•	•	•	✓	•	•	•
Sladeara (Slad.)	•	•	•	✓	•	•	•	•
Sophrocattleya	•	•	•	•	✓	•	•	•
Sophrolaelia (Sl.)	•	•	•	•	✓	•	•	•
Sophrolaeliocattleya (Slc.)	•	•	•	•	✓	•	•	•
Sophronitis (Soph.)	•	•	•	•	✓	•	•	•
Spathoglottis (Spa.)	•	•	✓	•	•	✓	•	•
Stamariaara (Stmra.)	•	✓	•	✓	•	•	•	•
Stanfieldara (Sfdra.)	•	•	•	•	✓	•	•	•
Stellamizutaara (Stlma.)	•	•	•	•	✓	•	•	•
Sutingara (Sut.)	✓	✓	•	✓	•	•	•	•
Teohara (Thra.)	✓	✓	•	✓	•	•	•	•
Trevorara (Trev.)	•	✓	•	✓	•	•	•	•
Trichoglottis (Trgl.)	•	•	•	✓	•	•	•	•
Trichonopsis (Trnps.)	•	•	•	✓	•	•	•	•
Trichopsis (Trcps.)	•	✓	•	✓	•	•	•	•
Trichostylis (Trst.)	•	•	•	✓	•	•	•	•
Trichovanda (Trcv.)	•	•	•	✓	•	•	•	•
Vanda (V.)	✓	✓	•	✓	✓	•	✓	•
Vandaenopsis (Vdnps.)	•	•	•	✓	•	•	•	•
Vandewegheara (Vwga.)	•	•	•	✓	✓	•	•	•
Vandofinetia (Vf.)	•	•	•	•	✓	•	•	•
Vandopsides (Vdpsd.)	•	•	•	✓	✓	•	•	•
Vandopsis (Vdps.)	•	✓	•	✓	•	•	•	•
Vandoritis (Vdts.)	•	•	•	•	✓	•	•	•
Vascostylis (Vasco.)	•	•	•	•	✓	•	•	•
Vaughnara (Vnra.)	•	•	•	•	✓	•	•	•
Wilkinsara (Wknsra.)	•	•	•	✓	✓	•	•	•
Yamadara (Yam.)	•	•	•	•	✓	•	•	•
Yapara (Yap.)	•	•	•	•	✓	•	•	•
Yoneoara (Ynra.)	•	✓	•	✓	•	•	•	•
Yusofara (Ysfra.)	•	✓	•	✓	•	•	•	•

Asia-Pacific Orchid Societies

AUSTRALIA
Orchid Society of the Northern Territory
P. O. Box 38493
Winnellie
NT 5789
Australia

Queensland Orchid Society (Inc.)
GPO Box 2002
Brisbane
Queensland
Australia 4001

HONG KONG
Hongkong Orchid Society
Room 610A Champion Building
301–309 Nathan Road
Kowloon
Hong Kong

INDONESIA
Perhimpunan Anggerik Indonesia
Jalan Bangka Raya No. 21
Jakarta
Indonesia

JAPAN
All Japan Orchid Society
c/o D. C. C., Shuwa Shiba Park Building
10F Shiba Koen, Minato-Ken
Tokyo 105
Japan

Japan Amateur Orchid Lovers' Association
29-9, 6-Chome, Seijo
Setagayu-ku
Tokyo
Japan

Japan Orchid Soceity
c/o Mr Akiyoshi Ohshima
15-8 Mefu 4, Chome Takerazuk
Hyogo-665
Japan

MALAYSIA
Johore
Johor Orchid Society
5 Jalan Nakhoda, Stulang Laut
80300 Johor Baru
Malaysia

Kedah
Persatuan Orkid Kedah
2367 Taman Lumba Kuda
05250 Alor Star
Kedah
Malaysia

Kelantan
Persatuan Orkid Kelantan
365 Kg Guchil
Jalan Bayam
1510 Kota Bahru
Kelantan
Malaysia

Melaka
Melaka Orkid Society
4832 Taman Anggerik
Klebang Kechil
75200 Melaka
Malaysia

Negeri Sembilan
Persatuan Orkid Negeri Sembilan
c/o 41F Rumah Kakitangan Tenaga Nasional
Kampong Gelam
71000 Port Dickson
Negeri Sembilan
Malaysia

Perak
Kelab Perhikaran Orkid
c/o 4 Pesiaran Gopeng 5
Taman Golf
31350 Ipoh
Perak
Malaysia

Perak Orchid Society
28 Jalan Building Society
Star Park
31400 Ipoh
Perak
Malaysia

Taiping Orchid Society
8 Creagh Road
Taiping 34000
Darul Ridzuan
Perak
Malaysia

Perlis
Persatuan Orkid Perlis
40B Jalan Besar
02600 Arau
Perlis
Malaysia

Petaling Jaya
Orchid Society of Selangor and Federal
Territory
P. O. Box 46
46000 Petaling Jaya
Malaysia

Persatuan Orkid Malaysia
P. O. Box 138
Petaling Jaya
Malaysia

Penang
Federation of Malaya Orchid Society
58 Lorong Mesra
Taman Keenways
14000 Bukit Mertajam
Pulau Pinang
Malaysia

Sabah
Sabah Orchid Society
c/o 3rd Floor
Block A Karamunsing
Jalan Tuaran
88300 Kota Kinabalu
Sabah
Malaysia

Sandakan Orchid Society
P. O. Box 81
90007 Sandakan
Sabah
Malaysia

NEW ZEALAND
North Shore Orchid Society
18 Little John's Street
Mount Roskill
Auckland
New Zealand

Taranaki Orchid Society
13A Veronica Place
Bell Block
Taranaki
New Zealand

PAPUA NEW GUINEA
Orchid Society of Papua New Guinea
P. O. Box 3367
Boroko
Papua New Guinea

PHILIPPINES
Philippines Orchid Society
163E De Los Santos Avenue, Mandaluyong
Metro Manila
Philippines

SINGAPORE
Nanyang Orchid Association
Bank of East Asia Building
137 Market Street #11-01
Singapore 0104

The Orchid Society of South East Asia
Robinson Road, P. O. Box 2363
Singapore 9043

SRI LANKA
Orchid Circle of Ceylon
82 5th Lane
Colombo 3
Sri Lanka

THAILAND
Orchid Society of Thailand
P. O. Box 953
Bangkok
Thailand

The Royal Horticultural Society of Thailand
77/3 Chaengwattana Road, Pak-Kred
Nonthaburi 11120
Thailand

USA
American Orchid Society
6000 South Olive Avenue
West Palm Beach
Florida 33405
USA

Hawaii Orchid Society
1710 Pali Highway
Honolulu
Hawaii 96813
USA

Pacific Orchid Society
P. O. Box 1091, Honolulu
Hawaii 96808
USA

Photographic Acknowledgements

The Editor and Publishers would like to thank the following for the use of their transparencies in this book. Every care has been taken to credit photographs correctly; Times Editions apologizes if any errors or discrepancies have occurred.

Yusof Alsagoff 10 top; 11; 12 all; 15; 16 bottom; 18; 21 top left, top right, centre left, centre right; 24; 26 top, bottom; 27 all; 29 bottom right; 30 top, bottom right; 31 centre; 32 bottom; 35 top right, bottom; 36 all; 37 second, third and bottom right; 38 all; 39 all; 40 all; 41 all; 42 all; 43 top, centre; 45 top, bottom; 46 centre, bottom; 47 centre; 48 bottom; 50 top, bottom right; 51 bottom left; 52; 55; 68 all; 71 bottom; 72; 73; 74; 76; 78 left; 79 all; 82; 84 left; 85 bottom left, top right; 88 top, bottom; 91 bottom; 95 top; 97; 99; 101 top, bottom; 102 bottom; 103 top; 108 all; 110 all; 111 bottom right; 112 all; 113 all; 116 top; 117 top; 120; 126; 133 top right, bottom left; 137 bottom right; 143 bottom right; 146 right; 147; 153 top left, top right; 161 bottom; 165; 166; 167; 175; 178; 179 top left, centre left; 180 bottom; 181 all except top left; 183 bottom right.

J. B. Comber 50 bottom left; 111 top right.

Myra Elliott 60, 61 all.

John Elliott 10 bottom; 16 top; 17 top; 22 bottom; 54; 56 all; 71 left; 78 right; 92 bottom left; 102 top; 104; 109 bottom; 138; 141 top; 144 top; 146 left; 149 bottom right; 183 bottom left.

Harold Johnson 62 all; 164.

David Lim 8; 17 bottom; 22 top; 28 bottom; 29 bottom left; 30 bottom left; 31 bottom; 32 top left; 33 all; 35 centre; 48 top; 75 top; 83; 84 right; 85 centre, bottom right; 89; 91 top; 92 top right; 94; 96 all; 100 all; 103 bottom; 106; 111 bottom left; 128 all; 129; 132 all; 133 bottom right; 148 bottom; 149 bottom left; 154; 158; 161 top; 162; 163; 174 all; 179 top right, bottom right; 180 top; 182.

Christopher Low K. W. 118; 183 top.

Low Kok Hing 150 top; 153 bottom left.

Phang Tuck Pew 34 top left; 37 top right; 134; 135.

Kiat Tan 28 top; 29 top; 75 bottom; 84 centre; 109 top; 111 top left; 114 all; 116 bottom; 117 bottom; 172; 181 top left.

Y. S. Phoon 44 top; 47 top, bottom; 98; 115; 179 bottom left.

Singapore Botanic Gardens 23 top; 34 top right, bottom; 43 bottom right; 44 bottom; 136 all; 137 bottom left, top right, centre right; 140; 141 bottom; 142 all; 143 centre, top; 144 centre, bottom; 148 top, centre; 149 top; 150 bottom; 153 bottom right; 169; 170.

Richard Sng 2; 31 top; 32 top right; 81; 87; 95 bottom; 107; 177; 180 centre.

Teoh Eng Soon 46 top; 86.

Yoke-Lan Wicks 119; 121; 123; 125.

Tim Yam 13; 21 bottom right; 23 bottom; 26 centre; 49 all; 51 top, bottom right; 70.

Gratitude is also due to Mr How Yee Peng, Mr Rodney Lim, and Mandai Orchid Gardens for permission to photograph plants and flowers.

Index

Numbers in italics refer to items shown in photographs and illustrations.

root
  active *56*
  dormant *56*
  rot 144, 151, 157
  structure 16–17, *16, 17*
rots 140–2, *140, 141, 142,* 151
Royal Horticultural Society (RHS) 20, 127, 182, 190

Sander's lists 20
Sappanara
  cultivation 67
Sappanara Ahmad Zahab *84*
scale insects 143–4, 148, *148,* 152, 156
Scelerotium rolfsii see basal rot
scented orchids 81
Schomburgkia
  cultivation 86–9
Scorpion Orchid *see* Arachnis
seasonal orchids 15, *15*
seeds 166–71, *167, 168, 169*
seedlings
  buying 127–8, *128, 129*
  growing 159–165, *160, 161, 162, 163, 164, 165*
shading 53–4, *54, 55*
  on balconies 122–3
shelving 120–1, *120*
shows 173–7, *177*
Singapore Botanic Gardens 23
Slipper Orchid *see* Paphiopedilum
slugs *148,* 149, *149,* 152, 156
snails *135,* 149, *149,* 152, 156
snow mould 143–4, 151, 157
sooty mould *82,* 143–4, 151, 157
Sophronitis
  cultivation 86–9
Sophronitis coccinea 87
Sophronitis grandiflora 87
Southern Blight *see* basal rot
sparrows 149, 152
Spathoglottis
  cultivation 48, 117
  unnamed hybrid *48, 62*
Spathoglottis affinis 117
Spathoglottis aurea 117, *117*
Spathoglottis plicata *48,* 117
species orchids
  cultivation 109–117
  definition 20, 133, *133*
Spider Orchid *see* Arachnis
spider mites *see* mites

spraying 154, *154*
squirrels 149, *149,* 152
Stamariaara Noel *85*
sterile culture techniques 23, 166–71
sunlight 53–4
  on balconies 122–3, *122*
sunscorch *153*
Swan Orchids *see* Cyanoches
sympodial orchids
  buying 131, *131*
  definition 10–11, *10,* 187
  main types 37–51
symptoms
  cultural faults 152–3, *153*
  diseases 151
  pests 152

terrestrial orchids
  cultivation 46–51
  definition 11
  potting 62–3, *62*
thrips 150, *150,* 152, 156
thumb pots 164–5
Tiger Orchid *see* Grammatophyllum speciosum
tissue culture 168–71, *168, 169, 170, 171*
Tobacco Mosaic Virus 136, 139
Trevorara
  cultivation 30–1
Trichoglottis ionosma 111
twisted growth *137*

Vandaceous quarter-terete hybrids
  cultivation 30–1
Vandaceous (strap-leaved) hybrids
  cultivation 34–5, 59, 70, 71
Vanda
  cultivation 30–1, 34–5
  repotting 80
  semi-terete 82–6
  strap-leaved 77–82
  multigeneric influence 75, *75*
  terete 25–8, 67, 74–7
  unnamed hybrids *34, 35, 79*
Vanda Alice Laycock 28
Vanda coerulea 34, *79,* 81
Vanda Cooperi 28
Vanda Dawn Nishimura 28
Vanda dearei 78, 86
Vanda dearei 'Orchidwood' *181*
Vanda Dicky Chua *83*